Prof Debashis Chatterjee is someone in whose life the two registers of action and thoughts meet. The reason why his writing appeals to the practitioners of learning is essentially because Debashis is the quintessential teacher, in fact, a miniature reflection of life itself.

—*Ameeta M Wattal, Principal, Springdales School, New Delhi*
Chairperson, National Progressive Schools' Conference

The experience was one of transformation from within. Enhancing the quality of thought and belief in the core values that govern human life, one is tempted to believe that you have to first lead yourself in the process of leading others.

—*Lata Vaidyanathan, Principal,*
Modern School, Barakhamba Road, New Delhi

Excellent and thought-provoking. It did move my cerebral molecules.

—*Maneesh Tripathi, Chief Executive Officer,*
Global Indian International Schools, Singapore

It was an eye-opener. We have not been given fish to eat; we have been taught how to fish.

—*Priyanka Bhatkoti, Principal,*
Maxfort School, Dwarka, New Delhi

DEBASHIS CHATTERJEE

CAN YOU TEACH A ZEBRA SOME ALGEBRA?

The Alchemy of Learning

wisdom tree

© Debashis Chatterjee
Illustrations by Tina Rajan

First published 2014

All rights reserved. No part of this book may be reproduced, stored in a retrieval system or transmitted in any form or by any means—electronic, mechanical, photocopying, recording or otherwise—without the prior permission of the author and the publisher.

ISBN 978-81-8328-373-1 (Hardback, The Class Act: Learn, Teach, Be)
ISBN 978-81-8328-371-7 (Paperback, Can You Teach a Zebra
 Some Algebra?)

Published by
Wisdom Tree
4779/23, Ansari Road
Darya Ganj, New Delhi-110 002
Ph.: 23247966/67/68
wisdomtreebooks@gmail.com

Printed in India

To
J Krishnamurti
and Those
Nameless Teachers of
My Universe Who Taught Me
How to Live

Preface

This book is about learning, teaching and being. Each moment of a human being's life can be a learning moment. Each step of ours can be a teaching step. All one has to learn to do is to be alert and aware.

Take this moment. Think of all that is happening in this moment. Perhaps a goat is eating a daily newspaper in Nairobi; a stock market tycoon is having a heart attack in Tokyo and a seasoned politician is playing a game of chess in Saudi Arabia. This very moment your heart is beating along with seven billion hearts. This very moment a lotus is blooming in New Delhi; one school kid may be shooting another with a gun in the inner city of New York. Your body is growing up, growing old and dying—this very moment. This moment is the womb of a universe of happenings and possibilities. Great teachers will tell you to meditate on this moment. Make this moment your God. You can learn all that you need to learn from this never ending *now-ness* of this moment.

Just as each moment is the source of all possibilities, each step you take is full of potential. Each step is like the whole universe tiptoeing upon itself. There is a universe inside you stepping on the universe outside you. The universe inside you is governed by the laws of psychology and physiology—patterns of thoughts and emotions, heart rate, breathing movements and the circulation of blood through millions of arteries and veins. The universe outside of you is governed by laws of gravitation, electricity and magnetism. To enable your foot to take a single step, the laws of your inner universe have to synchronise with the laws of the outer universe. It has taken human body millions of years to evolve before we could learn to walk on our two feet. Hidden in that one step of yours is the effort of a billion struggling and faltering steps of your ancestors. Do you remember those words of Neil Armstrong as he landed on the moon, 'That's one small step for man, one giant leap for mankind.' My teachers taught me to watch my steps as I walked. Their lessons were with me every step of the way like a banyan tree sheltering me from the hot sun.

Incidentally, I was born on September 5—the day India celebrates as Teachers Day. Although I began my life in the corporate world, I drifted to teaching as my calling. Today I do not see teaching as a profession but rather, as a way of celebrating life. You have the privilege of touching so many lives. The mission of teaching rewards you with unexpected gifts. I often meet my former students at airports in many cities of the world. Unexpectedly, some of them show up in morning newspapers, coffee shops and in movie halls. One such student of mine was Manjunath on whose life and death a film is made. Having been a witness to a life of inspiration that has now become a story, having interacted with the indelible spirit as a teacher, has been a bigger award than any other. In one leadership seminar class that I was teaching at the Harvard University's Kennedy School of Government, I stood awestruck and humbled as the former prime ministers of Canada and Finland and the president of Ecuador sat in my class as eager students. That was the moment that I remembered the words of one of my own teachers, my grandmother, 'A king is worshipped inside his own land, wisdom is worshipped everywhere.'

In this book I see the world through the vision given to me by many teachers. My teachers had different personalities. Some were quiet, others very talkative. There were some teachers who were great in their craft. Some were very ordinary. One learnt from all of them—perhaps not the same things.

In any case, the journey of learning begins with a teacher. Many teachers I know are obsessed with the curriculum. Between curriculum and the brain state of the learner, I prefer to look at the brain state of the learner. Curriculum is important but before you design the curriculum, you have to pay attention to the inner world of the child that you are teaching. This is not about covering the syllabus but about discovering the child. Greatness has to be discovered and nurtured. Every Alexander needs a Socrates. Every Chandragupta needs a Chanakya. Why? Because we all need our missing halves to fulfil ourselves. The day needs the night to refresh itself through sleep. The night needs the day to awaken to the world of new possibilities. When you are immature, you want maturity to be by your side. When you are too mature, you need somebody adventurous and innocent to be with you to learn how to mature. When you have a restless Arjuna, you need stabilising wisdom of Krishna. When you have a Krishna, you need an Arjuna to awaken and arise to act on that wisdom. So these complementarities have to come together—like day and night; spring and winter. A teacher can bring that missing touch in the evolving life of a student.

Much more than the curriculum, you need teachers who understand the mind of the student. Nobody recruits a teacher today for being kind. But being kind is very critical for learning. You see this all the time. Kindness is about empathy. Empathy is about understanding others as they are. We don't learn anything from a teacher who does not understand us. A teacher who does not understand us cannot teach us. All these are critical virtues that qualify one to be a good teacher.

This book asks what seems like a silly question—can you teach a zebra some algebra? You may in turn ask, what kind of a question is that? How can one teach algebra to a zebra? However, that is exactly what the education system we have inherited is attempting to do. Teachers go on to teach a subject with very little knowledge of the real subject—the student. Our schools remind me of the story of a sports school for animals. Here the teacher is employed to train animals to compete for Animal Olympics. The teacher looks at a rabbit and teaches it to fly. Then he gets hold of an eagle and forces the bird to run. The elephant is asked to swim and the tortoise is advised to practice a high jump. Finally after the training is over, the duck is declared the Olympic champion. Why? The duck can do a little bit of hopping, flying, jumping and swimming—a jack of all trades and master of none. Think of what's happening in our schools today. Students, like the duck in the story are asked to do a bit of everything with no deep knowledge of anything.

Our education system is pushing students towards increasing mediocrity. A star footballer in school is going through the grind of a coaching class to enter the IIT. A technology freak in IIT is grinding his way to join the IIM in search of a blue-chip job. An IIM pass out has to quit a life-sucking job as investment banker because she discovers one day that her original passion was to be a teacher in school. Yet, true education is about achieving mastery—it is about perfecting ourselves as a species in our unique way. How do we do that? By paying attention to the genius in each one of us. The word 'genius' is derived from Latin, *gignere* which means 'to give birth to' or 'to bring into being, create, produce'. Each one of us was created in our unique human shape and form. We were not mass manufactured in a factory. Our mission is life is therefore to create and to give birth to our true genius—something that we are born to do.

Mothers help us with our natural birth. Teachers help us to be twice born. The first birth is the gift of the universe to us; the second birth is our gift to the universe. This book will provide you with many refreshing ideas and several action choices as parents, students and teachers. I hope that the words that follow will in some way enrich your teaching, learning and being. Happy reading!

LEARN.
TEACH.
BE.

There is a difference between a
LEARNED MAN
and a man of learning.
A learned man is tied to the knowledge of the past.
A man of learning
is curious about the present.

The Ear Specialists

Ancient wisdom has long taught us that the tongue has just one customer—the ear. The masters were all ear specialists—they had a sharp ear that helped them distinguish between verbal gas and vital truth. They would listen with their eyes half closed, like contented cats, and quickly jump to attention just when the speaker's voice became noise. Listening gurus can separate the noise from the essence of the message. Modern communication experts tell us that in order to be heard, a message must be repeated several times. In my opinion that's not good communication at all. That's just nagging. Why would you repeat a message if you have delivered it well in the first instance? Chances are you have not developed a 'good ear' that makes the essence of your message clear.

How does one develop a good ear? Mystics have certified that there is 'an ear within the ear'. With the first ear you listen to such office fizz as 'our organisation's mission' or 'safety procedure briefings', or some such routine information. You tend to listen with your 'inside ear' when your colleague compliments you on your presentation or when you are afraid that your boss is about to fire you. Mastery springs from the inside ear job. An untrained ear hears what it just wants to hear. A trained ear hears the unheard and the unsaid.

A wonderful Chinese parable called 'The Sound of the Forest' describes the lessons learned by a young prince named T'ai in China in the third century AD. The parable is as follows:

King T'sao sent his son Prince T'ai to the great Master Pan Ku to learn the basics of good leadership. When the prince arrived before the master, he was advised to go alone into the Ming-Li Forest and return to the master after one year and describe the sound of the forest to him.

After spending months in the forest, when Prince T'ai returned, Pan Ku asked him to describe all that he could hear. The prince replied, 'I could hear the cuckoos sing, the leaves rustle, the hummingbirds hum, the crickets chirp, the grass blow, the bees buzz, and the wind whisper and holler...' Even before the prince could finish, the master told him to go back to the forest and find out what more he could hear.

Puzzled by his master's whims, Prince T'ai returned to the forest again. For days, he heard no sounds other than the ones he had heard before. Then, one morning, as he sat silently beneath the trees, he started to be conscious of the faint sounds he had never heard before. The more keenly he listened, the clearer the sounds became. Slowly, a new light of wisdom dawned upon him and he decided it was time to return to Pan Ku.

Upon his return, the master asked the prince what more he had heard. The prince responded with reverence, 'I could hear the sound of flowers opening, the sound of the sun warming the earth and the sound of the grass drinking the morning dew.' Master Pan Ku was delighted that his disciple had found the secret of the forest and said, 'To hear the unheard is necessary to be a good leader.'

Ananda is the Core of Learning

We all owe it to them—this fast vanishing breed that we call gurus. I had several in my life. The one who lingers most in my memory rarely explained anything. He just lived the teaching. He was a 'substitute teacher', which meant that he could walk into any class when the regular subject teacher was absent. He would impart lessons that sometimes had nothing to do with the subject and yet everything to do with the real subject—the student. He was truly expressive—when he frowned, he frowned with his entire face and when he laughed, you could see almost all of his surviving teeth, including the gold fillings inside his decaying molars.

He could make the most mundane lessons magical. His chemistry classes were an audio-visual treat. He would bring a complex chemical reaction alive, using imagery as deft as a painter's brush strokes.

A lot of teachers underestimate the impact of their words on the lives of their students. The words of a teacher have a potency that can shift the trajectory of a whole generation. One such expression that hit me hard was something that one teacher used often, 'Devote your life to matters of consequence.' Something that was not a matter of consequence for him was excessive analysis. 'Do not live too much inside your head,' he would say. If a student did not understand a particularly complex lesson, he would find ways to recast the lesson to make sure that the students understood.

My guru believed that learning is largely about instilling confidence of the student in his or her own ability. To the best of his students he would throw the most challenging problems. The more they racked their brains to decode the problems, the more they grew in confidence as learners. I realised that a brain that was dulled by the predictable was not suitable for learning. Predictable patterns, predictable events put the brain on the sleep mode. Great teachers have an uncanny ability to awaken those dormant aspects of our brain by asking the most unexpected questions. They teach us that this awakening happens not in the length of our answers but in the depth of our questions. One such question that I can spend a lifetime pondering on is, 'If livelihood is for life, what is life for?' My guru taught me to see the unity of life. He said, 'If all the oceans of the earth dried up, you will see one land mass in a seamless unity and not different countries.' An average teacher divides learning into an either/or universe; either socialist or capitalist, art or technology. But a great teacher would say, 'Look at a bamboo tree and observe that it is the most artistic piece of technology that draws water like a pump without polluting the environment. In a bamboo, art and technology come together.' A great teacher does not take sides; he brings the sides together. A guru is someone who gives us a vision of the whole.

My most 'learningful' moments with my guru were the most delightful moments. Most teachers don't seem to remember that delight, ananda, is the core of the learning process. Those are the eureka moments that liberate the mind. All learning is the pursuit of happiness that lies buried within us. My guru would often quote Arthur Schopenhauer, the German philosopher, who very aptly said, 'It is difficult to find happiness within oneself, but it is impossible to find it anywhere else.'

A Learned Teacher Can Put a Whole Nation to Sleep

One of my teachers who used to teach Research Methodology had a strange habit. After each class, he would tear off his class notes and throw them in the waste paper basket. When I asked him why he did so, he said, 'If I don't tear off the notes, I will tend to repeat what I know today in tomorrow's class. That will put me and the whole class to sleep. What I would learn tomorrow will keep me as well as the class awake.'

There is a difference between a learned man and a man of learning. A learned man is tied to the knowledge of the past. A man of learning is curious about the present. A learned man is bent over with the dead wood of knowledge, like an aging tree. A man of learning is vibrant and inquisitive, like a green twig breaking out of the soil after the rains. How often are teachers in the learning mode?

A learned man can put not just a whole class but a whole

generation to sleep. He has all the answers and no room in his head for new questions or discoveries. He can tell the distance between planet Earth and Mars, but he cannot take you on the journey from your head to your heart. Learning is about integration of the head and the heart. Haven't we often heard our teachers urging us to 'learn by heart'. Obviously, they were not referring to the biological mechanism called the heart. The expression 'learning by heart' refers to deepening of attention by going to the centre of our awareness. When someone talks about himself in the first person singular 'I', he often points his finger towards the heart rather than the head or the stomach. By Nature's design, he points towards the centre of his awareness. A teacher's primary job is to awaken the urge to concentrate on this centre of awareness—this is the core of all learning. Swami Vivekananda was a prodigious learner who was known to have memorised a whole book after reading it just once. He had once said, 'The world is ready to give up its secrets if we only know how to knock, how to give it the necessary blow. The strength and force of the blow come through concentration. There is no limit to the power of the human mind. The more concentrated it is, the more power is brought to bear on one point; that is the secret.'

Can You Learn from Someone Who Can't be Taught?

I have had the privilege of learning from some very dedicated students of mine. One of them is Sandip Yuwanati who graduated from my class at the Indian Institute of Management, Lucknow. Sandip once told this story in one of my classes:

The story is about an Indian gurukul—an institution that was well known for graduating excellent teachers. Over the years, this institution had built a reputation for itself as a great learning place.

The school head was an extraordinarily gifted master. His name was Guru Mahesh. He was loved and respected by his colleagues and students for his phenomenal teaching skills. One of the students of Guru Mahesh was Subodh. Guru Mahesh knew that Subodh had a lot of promise to be a great teacher. So he advised Subodh to go and teach some of his students residing in the gurukul. Subodh followed his master's instructions and did an excellent job. He got even better ratings than Guru Mahesh from the students. Subodh was ecstatic but slightly embarrassed that he had outshone his own guru. He did not realise, however, that Guru Mahesh had given him the best students who were quick learners. Mahesh himself had taken on the challenge of teaching the less gifted students. The success of Subodh was therefore largely due to the quality of students he had, as compared to his guru. When asked to comment on Subodh's eligibility to be his rightful successor in the gurukul, this is what Guru Mahesh said, 'Subodh is a brilliant person and good teacher but this incident does not mean that he is a better teacher than Kamal is. Kamal, who is a former student, is the one person who I think is not only a better teacher than I am, but also perhaps the most gifted teacher we have had in a long time.'

Some of the students narrated this incident and Guru Mahesh's comment back to Subodh, who got very disappointed and felt dejected. He could not comprehend as to how Guru Mahesh had decided that Kamal was better than him without giving him any chance of competing against Kamal. Finally, he decided to take this matter to Guru Mahesh and told him that he had never ever compared himself to him and would never do that in future...but he wanted to know on what basis had Guru Mahesh given the verdict that Kamal was better than him.

Guru Mahesh just kept silent.

He thereafter sent Subodh on a tougher assignment. He asked Subodh to teach some illiterate students in a nearby city. These students were school dropouts, but very rich.

One of them was a cobbler, the other was a potter and the third, a barber. But these three illiterates were not normal individuals. In spite of having a cavalcade of servants and a large number of employees, these three people would never miss a single day in their work schedule.

They would in fact go to their workplace and start working with their employees. Now the real challenge began for Subodh. When he left the gurukul for this assignment, he had thought that it was a rather easy task Guru Mahesh had given him. He could teach the brightest minds, what was the big deal in teaching the ordinary illiterates?

With utmost enthusiasm, he reached the city and met Hariram, the barber. During a conversation with Hariram, he realised that he could not make him literate as easily as he had thought of. So he tried to convince Hariram. He explained how being literate would help him in his trade. He tried to convince him about the social benefits he would derive out of his literacy. But all in vain—Hariram said he already had whatever education and literacy he needed to run his business.

The other two illiterates also gave him the same response. Subodh tried every trick of persuasion. But all his efforts were an utter waste. Guru Mahesh had given him three months to accomplish the task. But by the end of the first month, Subodh realised that he wouldn't be able to teach those illiterates even a single sentence. Such was their stubborn refusal to learn anything from a gurukul teacher!

Very reluctantly, Subodh packed his bags and got back to

the gurukul at the end of the first month itself. Crestfallen, he went to Guru Mahesh and told him that he was not able to teach anything in his new assignment. After listening to his ordeal, Guru Mahesh consoled him saying he should not feel dejected. He added, 'In fact I myself would not be able to do it. Even Kamal failed to teach them a single word.'

Hearing this, Subodh raised a question, 'If Kamal could not do it, you yourself agree that you won't be able to do it; then how come Kamal is still a better teacher than me?'

Now Guru Mahesh smiled broadly and said, 'Do you want to know why Kamal would be better than you or me; or for that matter, all of us? Do you want to know what Kamal did?' Subodh was very curious to know. So, Guru Mahesh continued, 'Kamal also realised that he won't be able to teach them, but he did not come back in one month like you did. He stayed there and when he came back after three months, he was an excellent cobbler, barber and potter. He could not teach them anything but he was able to utilise the time to learn from them. This is an exceptional ability...to learn from others. Kamal's passion for learning is tremendous; he can learn even from illiterates. That's the extent of his curiosity which makes him a genius of the highest order. There are teachers who wouldn't care so much about their personal successes or failures. They would just immerse themselves in learning. They, like Kamal, would always be the most gifted teachers of this gurukul.'

Flexibility + Expertise = Flexpertise

I was in Singapore in the middle of a flu scare. If there is any country in the world where you can expect to be flu screened to perfection, it has to be this incredible island. The Silk Air Flight transported us from sleepy Kochi to Singapore early in the morning. While driving from Changi, I realised that the bougainvilleas in the middle of the road had grown more flirtatious and flamboyant than when I had visited Singapore last.

I was invited in the city to speak at an international conference of 1400 school principals from almost forty counties. In my conference kit I had, among other things, a digital thermometer and bottles of disinfecting soap—a reminder that this life is as unpredictable as the flu itself. One could not help wondering how, with all our knowledge of zoology, genetics, anatomy, high speed computing and rocket science, we were still vulnerable to the unknown yet flimsy flu virus.

One of my concerns in this conference was—how far does

our education prepare us for the unknown? We live in the maze of a systems world of button pushing and predictable responses. Our world is one of expertise and extreme specialisation. In the systems world, we are driven to distraction by a swarm of data—handphone number, that elusive plumber; dates of delivery, pangs of expiry; bills to be paid and plans to be laid. We are transfixed by trivia and mesmerised by multimedia. The real educators of our young and impressionable are not classroom teachers but those ad film-makers who catch restless eyeballs more readily than the unglamorous blackboards. Education today is more about digitised fantasy than about reality.

Education of tomorrow has to prepare our kids to deal with the unforeseen of tomorrow. In a rapidly changing world, we need education that will help us deal with reality that is changing quicker than what all our man-made systems together can grasp.

What kind of expertise do we need to cope with the world out there? In the conference, Prof David Perkins of Harvard Education School used the term 'flexpertise' to describe flexible ways of applying our expertise to real life.

He asked how many of the principals had learnt the quadratic equation in school—predictably many hands went up. Then, he bent over and asked, 'How many of you still use the quadratic equation?' Many hands dropped down. Then the veteran Harvard guru asked the final clinching question, 'How many of you still use the quadratic equation outside the workplace?' Virtually no hand was visible.

We all know what happens to us when we have all the expertise in the world but not the flexibility of mind to apply this expertise outside our domain of specialisation. So Prof Perkins had it right. We need 'flexpertise' at a time when all our expertise while working to solve a very narrow band of problems does not work any more. Problems of education are interrelated. Fragmented solutions can become problems in themselves. Curriculum, societal values, parental mindset, a student's motivation to learn, teacher's skill, evaluation methods, test scores—these are all interconnected issues. If you want to improve test score of a student without attending to his motivation to learn, you will not succeed. Solving one problem in isolation does not solve the other.

We learnt in the conference that the goals of education are to teach for understanding; to help students learn to use knowledge to solve unexpected problems rather than simply recite back facts; and to develop a culture of thinking in the classroom so that students think critically and creatively. The primary skill worth learning is reflective thinking which involves the flexible and active use of knowledge.

It was a veritable feast of ideas sharing in the conference. An eminent educator quizzed me, 'How are you dealing with the flu in God's own country, India?'

I said, 'We are doing the usual stuff like screening viruses, may not be as well as Singapore does. But then, we Indians have an ample supply of an antivirus called faith.'

'What does faith mean to you?' he asked, quite amused by my response.

I said, 'Faith like "flexpertise" is mightier than the flu. While the flu can keep you awake all night long, faith makes a comfortable bed. Faith is a form of education through which your heart holds on to one answer even when the mind raises many questions.'

Faith in a teacher's ability is an important issue in learning for a student. Very often, parents undermine their child's faith in the teacher by being critical of the teacher at home when the child is listening in. The child begins to dislike the teacher through this process. Just think of this—have we really ever learnt anything worthwhile from a teacher we have disliked?

Expertise to Excellence

Would you trust a dentist who has the best expertise and most modern surgical instruments to pull out your rotting molar tooth? Perhaps yes. Would you still trust the dentist if he was known to be a little absent-minded and the chances were, even if one in a thousand, that he might pull the wrong tooth out? Perhaps...you would think twice. I was recently invited to a very well regarded medical college of India as the chief guest for their annual convocation. While preparing for my talk, I was wondering what would make an expert medical practitioner an excellent doctor. The answer I found was this—the quality of the mind.

I told the few hundred graduating medical students that the most precious diagnostic instrument that a doctor possessed was not a brain scanner or a laser knife but an excellent mind. Yet, how many doctors really did something to study their own mind? There was a hush of recognition in my audience of bright young women and men.

As experts, we are paid to solve problems. The more complex the problem, the greater is the expertise demanded. But the most persistent problems we face defy the greatest of expertise. Our most persistent problems could range from intestinal disorders to a dispute at an international border.

Whether intestinal or international, it is in the mind that the problem takes shape. Habitual eating and drinking patterns, with no awareness of what we are eating and when, can lead to chronic stomach tantrums. International border disputes are caused by the same unawareness of the human mind. Such a mind lapses into habitual patterns of thoughts and behaviour.

An Israeli was asked how he would discuss peace with an Arab cab driver. The Israeli responded, 'I will shake hands with him. Then, I will hug him and start talking to him politely about the importance of peace in the region. Then, I will beat him and beat him until he talks peace with me.'

Where expertise fails, the quest for excellence begins. Excellence often begins with examination of our own minds. You can start your journey in excellence by a simple practice that I have found very useful. At the end of a day, I bring my awareness to revisit the whole day in reverse chronological order—starting with the last half an hour and ending with the time I got up from bed. It is like pressing the rewind button of a mental movie. I often discover many moments in the day that I have been completely unaware of. Often I discover words that should not have been spoken or assumptions that should not have been made. Sometimes, I discover moments of genuine happiness in the course of the day that escaped my awareness then. Initially you may find this exercise challenging. But once you master it, you are bound to have a clearer mind at the end of the exercise. The story that illustrates this point has now become part of the medical school folklore:

A veteran urologist is demonstrating how to sample urine to a class of medical students. He reaches out towards each sample, dips a finger in the bottle, raises his hand to the mouth and licks it. The students find this repulsive but have no choice but to repeat the instructor's example when they are invited to do so.

At the end of the class the instructor tells the students, 'While I can't fault you for your general expertise in sampling urine, I must say that you have been very poor observers. If you were a little more aware, you would have noticed that while I dipped my middle finger in the bottle of the urine sample, I only sucked on my index finger while pretending to taste the urine. Class over.'

Expertise is about qualification and experience. Excellence is about quality of mind and awareness. Professional excellence is a result of developing a quality mind through constant awareness. A lot of experts I know have almost blind allegiance to their expertise. Experts tend to think of themselves as those who have finally reached their goal. Those in pursuit of excellence are always beginners. Excellence is a journey without a finish line. It begins everyday with a new awakening and a new insight that enriches the mind. Come, let's begin.

Creativity—The New Name for Literacy

Creativity, one hears, is the new form of literacy. We are born immensely creative and continue to be so until we go to school. Our schools do the best they can to check us out of our creative ways. Books are like walls and different subjects resemble apartments that insulate us from inseparable lives that breathe inside these walls. If books could hold conversations with each other and subjects could mingle like the noodles of neurons in our brains, going to school would be fun indeed. Instead, there is a worldwide caste system prevalent in schools that pushes down creative arts to the bottom of a pile of subjects, dominated by science and mathematics at the very top. Just think of this—no phenomenon in Nature separates science and mathematics from art and aesthetics. The separation between science and the arts exist only in our information stuffed heads!

Our creative spark originates in a phenomenon that I would like to describe as 'no-thing-ness'. Creativity rarely comes from having more things around us. On the contrary, when a creative artist transforms a piece of wood into a marvellous statue what she actually does is dematerialise wood into 'no-thing-ness'. She does this by chiselling away bits and pieces of this material thing called wood as she carves out the aesthetic value of 'no-thing-ness'. The creative process is the art and science of bringing forth something out of nothing. That is why the greatest of creative works come out of constraints and oftentimes from the absence of material resources.

If creativity is 'not-a-thing', what is it then? Is it a thought? No. Creativity is not a thought either. However, creativity may eventually express itself through new thought processes. If I were to imagine our world in 2045 when our MBA students would officially retire—I wonder if my current thoughts and teachings would still be relevant for them? Our conditioned thought processes from the past cannot create a future scenario even for the next three years, let alone 2045. We will know nothing about our future unless we participate in the random and unpredictable creative processes through which our future is being shaped. The future cannot be thought through by referring to the past. The future has to be reimagined. Where thoughts fail, imagination takes over. Strangely, our schools do so little to kindle the child's creative imagination. My Strategy professor would evoke the imagination in a way that was particularly fascinating. He usually dressed in a white shirt. He would take a particular stand on a debatable topic. Then he would go out of the class for a few minutes and come back and take a polar opposite stand to the one he had taken earlier. But, the most remarkable thing about his turnaround was that when he came back to class the second time to argue against himself, he would change his white shirt to a black shirt. This stark visual contrast made him such a memorable teacher.

The randomness and unpredictability of our universe is the real creative source. Quantum physicists call this the uncertainty principle. In simple language, this is the principle of 'no-thing-ness' and 'no-thought-ness'. We can't think through anything with absolute precision until it happens. Creative geniuses do not predict the universe they live in; they just help create it by complete absorption in the creative process. The finest managerial decisions come from complete absorption in the decision-making process! A heart surgeon does the most unorthodox procedure of a heart surgery in a creative flash of insight when he is totally focussed on the surgery. A great footballer scores a goal from the near impossible angle when he is playing in the 'zone'. It happens when the player becomes the play.

Our schools can teach students to be creative by first understanding that creativity can never be taught. A teacher can only help students hone their creative capacity by giving them enough unstructured reflection time to be totally absorbed in something with heads, hands and hearts. If creativity is like the flow of nothingness, innovation is the process of harnessing this flow to get something useful out of nothing. A creative idea may not automatically lead to innovation. Just think of this: 98 per cent of the creative ventures in Silicon Valley do not survive till the second year of their operation. Innovation demands taking a creative insight through the complex web of interaction and interrelationships until the idea becomes usable. Gandhi's creative idea of winning freedom through non-violence became one of the world's greatest social innovations. This happened because Gandhi persisted in living and acting on this idea. He also engaged in countless social interactions to embed this idea amongst millions of Indians. Innovation is creativity + action + interaction. Great organisations like Sony, Gillette, Google and 3M fight their corporate battles not just by creative strategies but by diligently climbing the high hills of innovation.

Just think of a class on energy. As a teacher, you can divide the class of thirty students into six groups. Each group represents a class of experts—scientists, artistes, politicians, farmers, industrialists and the last group represents meditating monks. Through their interaction, you are more likely than not to get a whole new perspective on energy.

Transmission Loss between Teaching and Learning

A fundamental truth about the teaching profession is that the circle of teaching for a teacher is complete only when the circle of learning for a student is complete. This means that a teacher may be very learned, yet the students in his class may not learn much at all. I have had a teacher who would appear in class like Hamlet mumbling monologues. The moment he entered the class, there would be a ripple of yawns from a large cross section of the students. While the class was on, they would pretend to blow noses, throw paper missiles at each other and even vigorously shake their wrists wondering if time had stood still inside their watches.

Between a well-intentioned teacher and a disappointed learner, there is a huge loss in transmission. This loss happens in the battlefield between the current of knowledge broadcast by the teacher and the resistance of succeeding generations of bored students. What gets lost in transmission is not just information, but also energy and enthusiasm for learning. A teacher who cannot connect with the learners is boring a generation to death. He is guilty of culpable homicide. If he is not killing them, he is creating permanent learning disabilities. Only a sensitive teacher can see the violence that is unleashed in our classrooms day in and day out. One way to prevent transmission loss between teaching and learning is to ask each student at the end of the class to prepare a note on what they learnt. They can then share their notes with each other in groups of four or five. This will ensure not just learning from the teacher but also from the peer group. Eric Mazur of Harvard University has devised a technique that involves a teacher posing a question to the whole class. First, the students are given some time to think about the question. Then the teacher asks them to discuss their answers with whoever is sitting next to them. After this, each student is asked to give their refreshed answers once again. Mazur found each student was able to get the answer in a couple of minutes. They also had greater confidence in their own ability.

The critical thing here is that the knowledge that a teacher possesses will have to cross the brain barrier of students in order for this frozen knowledge to begin to flow through the minds and hearts of learners.

Routine is Important; Rotting is Not

Nothing defines you more than a day in your life. In one way, a day is like a perpetual prison. In the course of a day, you enter into a jail of your habituation. Just consider your typical day—brushing your teeth, rushing through a shower, browsing a newspaper, brewing coffee, chewing breakfast, a comatose commute to your place of work, an encounter with your boss, shuffling papers, ruffling tempers, commuting back home, watching a soap, cuddling your pet before finally hitting the bed. Incidentally, in this time prison of your own making you are both the jailor and the jailed.

Now consider another day that you choose for yourself—getting up a good half hour before you usually do, brushing your teeth with the wrong hand, reading a section of the newspaper you usually don't, skipping coffee for a beverage that you loved as a kid, making your own breakfast, doing a few more stretches, walking to work, presenting your boss a book that he might like to read, deciding that you will not judge anybody in the office, buying some yellow roses on your way back home, coming out to your balcony to watch the sunset, taking a bath with your favourite instrumental music turned on, viewing television with the sound muted, reading yourself to sleep with an inspiring book.

A day can burn or bore you out. When you drag yourself through the rut of a routine life, you are likely to douse the flame of your enthusiasm. Routine is important; rotting is not. When was the last time you learnt something for the first time? I know a doctor who fell in love and learnt to dance a salsa for the first time when he was nearly seventy years old! Alongside the rigour of routine, you require a ritual of renewal. Why? If you look around in Nature, you will see that life is never linear. A burst of activity in Nature is always followed by a bout of relaxation. Life in Nature is circular—changing seasons, waxing and waning of the moon, shifting constellation of stars—all of these point towards the urge for renewal and rejuvenation.

In a human being, energy moves in non-linear ways. Our attention is the primary source of our energy. You can hold your attention intensely on a subject for about ninety minutes or so. After that your concentration is likely to flag. Desire is another source of energy. Whatever we deeply desire will energise us to pursue the object of our desire. This pursuit has to be punctuated with necessary diversion. Can you kiss someone for hours without wanting to do anything else, however desirable that kiss may be? Moderation is critical to management of human energy.

Moderation involves slowing down, pacing ourselves to be in sync with the rhythms of our energy.

Our emotions are deep sources of our energy. If you observe the energy associated with your emotions, you will realise that there is a waxing and waning in the movement of emotions. How long at a stretch can you feel anger or affection for someone? An hour? Two hours? You will discover that the emotions of anger and affection come and go like night and day. Emotions are energy bubbles in motion. You have to be an observer of the course of your emotions in a whole day. From the observatory that is located inside you, you will see a constellation of emotions. You will discover that anger, fear, happiness, lust, jealousy—all emerge in a pattern in the course of a day.

Take all the sixteen odd hours of waking time in a day. Divide those sixteen hours into your typical energy chunks! You will find out that you feel deeply energised during some parts of the day and thoroughly depleted of energy and enthusiasm during the rest. How do you live the rest of your day like the best of your day? Isn't today the first day of the rest of your current life? You have been given this on rent. How will you express your thankfulness to the giver? You are not fully certain that you will wake up alive inside the same room that you will go to bed in? Not everyone in our world will wake up tomorrow on this beautiful earth? With this realisation, how will you choose to live today? Just think it over before you seize the day!

Hoarding Knowledge like Property

Many organisations in the world describe their wealth in the form of knowledge capital. It makes one feel that knowledge is some kind of real estate that needs to be fenced in by organisational boundaries.

Hoarding knowledge as though it is property kills the spirit of learning. Learning is not about accumulation but about accommodation of knowledge. Learning is the art of creating space so that the learner can see the movement of knowledge in space and time. Knowledge of yesterday may not be relevant today. Knowledge of the past may not be relevant to the future. Knowledge used properly and appropriately, is learning. Knowledge should never be hoarded. It should rather be used like a disposable tissue. You don't cling on to a tissue paper after you have wiped your nose with it, do you? The movement of open source learning across the world today tells us that learning like love cannot be divided. Learning can only be multiplied and shared.

Covering Curriculum or Discovering the Learner?

Covering the curriculum is a perennial obsession that teachers have. This is like a still photographer trying to capture the journey of a flying plane inside the lens of a camera. The lens only captures a small image of the plane—it cannot really cover the entire dynamism of a huge jet plane roaring through the air. Learning is like a jet plane moving up against gravity and the resistance of the atmospheric conditions. You have to be inside the plane to experience some of that. Teachers who are only hung up on the curriculum do not quite experience the thrill and adventure of teaching or learning. They are like a still photographer trying to capture learning from the outside.

To use another familiar example, the curriculum is like the menu card in a restaurant. Discovery of the learner is like eating the dish you ordered from the menu. The proof of a pudding is not in the description of it in the menu. The proof is in the tasting of it.

Once a teacher samples the enchantment that is inside the learner, she has truly discovered the learner. Once the curiosity of the learner is evoked by the teacher, the curriculum is spontaneously covered. Great teachers have a rare knack of managing the flow of curiosity in the class. One of them teaching the history of India to standard VII students taught about emperor Akbar by saying that 'Akbar became emperor at the age of eleven. If he was alive today, he would be a class VII student—he was of the same age as you are now. Now imagine if you were made an emperor. You can also be like Akbar.' By this time all the students were hooked to the teacher's narrative as she continued, 'You know Akbar was more interested in horse riding than in his studies—just like many of you are.' Needlessly to say, Akbar was brought alive to her class by this influential teacher. Another way a teacher can evoke the curiosity among students is by ending the class with a question rather than an answer.

Multiple Choice Mind Versus Choiceless Awareness

Generations of learners grew up ticking boxes or bubbles. The era of multiple choice 'objective type' tests spread like chickenpox across continents. The ease with which the ticked sheets could be computed by an examiner or a computer made these tests popular among teachers. Multiple choice tests helped not so much the learning ability of students but the testing capability of the examiners. Examination became a law unto itself. Multiple type tests were divorced from learning.

The prospect of having to choose from many options makes the mind restless. Like the multiple branches of a tree fragment the tree trunk, multiple choices in the mind fragment awareness. The mind becomes indecisive when confronted with too many choices. Think of someone who surfs one hundred odd channels on television to decide which programme she wants to see. Compute the time she has wasted to reduce her options from one hundred channels to the two or three that she really wants to watch. Then observe how she flips channels again between the two or three that she has zeroed in on. By constantly fragmenting her attention, the channel surfer reduces the quality as well as the quantity of engagement with the channel she really wants to see.

A multiple choice mind is a monkey mind. It has become a compulsive, addictive chooser. This is a dangerous development from the learning point of view. Learning requires freedom. Yet having a choice is not the same as being free. Learning happens when we can observe reality around us without the compulsion of having to choose. This compulsion distorts reality based on our likes and dislikes. We may go to a supermarket and choose to buy some from a plethora of stuff we like irrespective of whether we need it or not.

What is the alternative to a multiple choice mind? One of India's enlightened teachers J Krishnamurti often used to talk about 'choiceless awareness'. Amitabh Bachchan, the great actor, told us a story of how as a young man he once vented his frustration on his father Harivansh Rai Bachchan when he was finding it difficult to get suitable employment. The angry young man shouted at his father, 'Why did you give birth to me when you cannot make me fit to be employed?' His father did not utter a word in reply. The next day, the junior Bachchan got a handwritten note from his father that read, 'God willing, you may have a son some day. Should this son of yours turn around to ask you whether you sought his permission before giving birth to him, what will your reply be?' The young Amitabh learnt that there are things in life we cannot really choose—like choosing our parents for example? Awareness that is not fragmented by choices transports us from a monkey to a meditative mind. In the state of choiceless awareness the learner can discover the freedom wherein, she can act decisively without the distortions caused by competing choices.

A Theory of Life

Every educator needs a theory of life. A theory is not something that is divorced from life. You can't learn about life by practice alone. For instance, you cannot say that I will learn about death by practising it. Nor can you say I will learn about Siamese twins by becoming the father of a couple of them—that would be quite impractical. Everyone who lives a meaningful life has some kind of a theory tucked inside his head. A school principal once told me that he believed in a short and cryptic theory of life that was contained in no more than a word—'thorough!' You could see his theory at work as he got up from his desk only after he had completed all that he had set out to do for the day.

Yet another teacher had a theory of life that went, 'If you can't beat them, join them.' You could measure the effectiveness of his theory based on how his students were so deeply engaged in his class.

A theory of life can evolve from your personal experience

or from a role model who has inspired you. This role model can be a historical figure or your friendly neighbourhood dentist. J Krishnamurti, himself an inspiring teacher, advised his friends and other teachers not to repeat his teachings—that would be propaganda. He advised them to live his message. J Krishnamurti never allowed his own photograph or statue to be worshipped by his followers. Take the example of another great teacher whom we all know as the Buddha. On his death bed Buddha's message to his favourite disciple Ananda was, 'Do not depend on any external means, be a light unto yourself—*Appo deepo bhava.*' When the message of a great teacher is fully assimilated in daily life, that message becomes a living truth. When a message is lived, a theory of life meets life itself.

We are Visual Ragpickers.

Great masters in the ancient civilisations were known as seers. The masters saw the world around them perceptively, not passively. Most of us would see a falling apple and think nothing of it. It takes the insight of an Isaac Newton to see beyond the event and discover the force of gravity. We all see suffering around us. Yet it takes the insight of Buddha to go to the root cause of human suffering and identify it as ceaseless desire.

We are visual ragpickers. In the ordinary state of consciousness, we passively pick up fragmented visual impressions of objects or events. This is a low energy activity, like mechanically picking up bits and pieces from our environment. High energy seeing involves not accumulating objects or events but something more. It involves the discipline of seeing through and beyond events, to the invisible processes that shape those events.

Seeing with New Eyes!

Try this experiment. Close your eyes for thirty seconds and visualise the word 'tree'. Observe any tree that appears on your mind's screen. Examine your mental picture down to the smallest detail. What do you see? A fir, a maple or a eucalyptus? A palm tree swaying in the breeze? Or did you see no tree at all? Did you see only the word 'tree' written on your mental map? Perhaps you saw the green leaves of the branch spreading like arteries. Perhaps you saw the tree trunk or some flowers. Now ask yourself this important question, 'Did I visualise the roots when thinking of a tree?' Ninety-nine people out of hundred will say, 'No'. But the roots, though invisible to you, do exist. Don't they? Indeed, the roots are the most important components of a tree. Yet why does our mind miss such an important portion of the tree while visualising it? I have been asking the same question to people around the world from different cultures and different countries. Why don't we visualise the roots of a tree? I receive more or less the same answer, 'Because we normally don't get to see the roots.' What does this tell us? It tells us two things. First, our thought becomes conditioned by our sense-based data of reality. Second, our thought can process reality only by dividing the indivisible. Simply speaking, our thought is incapable of seeing the entire picture. Thought sees everything in fragments and hence it cannot comprehend the essential unity of life in Nature.

Those of us who teach have to look at the tree of learning with new eyes. We have to learn to see the invisible roots of this tree that is as old as our human civilisation. Education has humanised men and women. Our first commitment as educators of the twenty-first century would be to preserve our humanity.

LEARN.
TEACH.
BE.

LEARNING
RARELY HAPPENS THROUGH A TEXT.
REAL LEARNING
HAPPENS IN CONTEXT.

I Can, Therefore I Teach

A geography teacher was asking the class to memorise this dubious lesson, 'Nile is a mountain that is situated in Egypt.' The headmaster, on hearing this, confronted the teacher and asked him if he really knew that Nile was a river and not a mountain. The teacher shot back saying, 'For the pittance of a salary I get, it does not matter whether Nile is a river or a mountain.' To cap it, he said, 'Nile will be transformed into a river as soon as my salary is raised.'

You get the picture. Unfortunately, teaching has become a kind of a pastime for some, rather than a passionate pursuit. A generation of teachers prods along, while they are looking for jobs that pay better. Yet, the most highly regarded leaders of human societies for centuries have been teachers. These teachers were the channels through which the DNA of human civilisation was transferred from one generation to another. If the Macedonian hero Alexander had a teacher in Aristotle, the

Indian king Chandragupta Maurya had a teacher in Chanakya. These teachers taught not because they could not do anything else, but because nothing else was more valuable to their societies than what these wise teachers taught.

Great teaching is more like a craft than a technique. To evoke curiosity in the learner, to care for the learner and to take the learner on a journey of discovery are some of the most critical elements of this craft. A memorable journey is not when you are forced to take the trip but when the trip takes you to those enchanting spaces that you have never visited before. One of my first teachers who herself never went to school, my grandmother, used to teach me through extraordinary stories. Here is a story she told me from the Indian epic, *The Mahabharata* that has remained with me for a long time:

Yaksha, a demigod, was having a Q&A session with Yudhisthira—the eldest of the five Pandava princes, who was known for his commitment to truth.

A set of questions of Yaksha to Yudhisthira was, 'What is the best of all laudable things? What is the most valuable of all possessions? What is the highest of all gains? And what is the best of all kinds of happiness?'

Yudhisthira responded, 'The best of all laudable things is skill; the best of all possessions is knowledge; the best of all gains is health; and contentment is the best of all kinds of happiness.'

Teachers bridge the gap between our past and our future. They anchor the values of our society. They ensure continuity of cultures in times of change. Teachers stitch together knowledge of generations into the tapestry of our times.

Can You Teach a Zebra Some Algebra?

Impossible! Why? The zebra, unlike you, does not have a developed intellect. Therefore, the zebra cannot hold the mind long enough on an idea or a thought to be able to learn something as abstract as algebra. The ability to hold the mind in one place for some length of time results in concentration. The entity that holds the scattered mind in one place and concentrates its energy is the intellect.

The intellect helps in the concentration of thought, of feeling or action around a given purpose. This concentration results in the firm fixing of the mind on one single point of attention. All distracting thoughts and emotions are kept away. Disturbance caused by the wandering senses are checked. In short, the intellect disciplines the mind in a way that it can access the higher powers of human consciousness.

Think of this. You wish to break a slice of brick made of hardened clay. If you hit the brick with each one of your five fingers, one at a time, the brick will not break. You will then draw your fingers in and concentrate their energies in the form of a fist. Chances are, when you hit the brick with your fist, the brick will be broken. Concentration converts a wish to a will. A wish is like a drifting cloud of thoughts and emotions. Will is as sharp as a ray of the sun. A steady flow of will breaks through thoughts, emotions that come in its way.

Concentration is the source of all knowledge. A scientist looking through a microscope is bringing his entire will to study a cell. An astronomer looking through a telescope brings his entire mental energy to gaze at a constellation of stars. Through concentration, the mind can also be turned back upon itself. This is a unique human capability through which we can learn about the secrets of our own mind—our intentions, our hidden emotions and our motives.

If you asked a zebra to study its own mind, it cannot do so—simply because its intellect has not been developed in a school. Therefore, the zebra's actions are based on its instincts rather than its concentrated will. The zebra for instance will not think before kicking somebody, 'Is it all right to kick him...how hard should I kick...is kicking someone good manners...?' Devoid of intellect, the zebra will just compulsively kick.

The most critical task for a teacher is therefore to help develop a student's intellect. A sharp intellect will give the student the power of discrimination which the zebra can never have. It will help the student navigate the world of uncertainties through willpower. This story will illustrate how a great teacher develops the intellect of a child:

The child shared with his teacher a dream that he had every night. In the dream he saw two wolves fighting. One wolf was bright, kind and compassionate. The other one was dark, mean and ruthless. 'Every night they fight in my dream,' said the kid, 'but, I want to know which one of these two wolves will finally win?'

If this was an ordinary teacher, the response would probably have been, 'The bright one will win and the dark one will lose.'

But this great teacher had an answer that would develop the child's intellect. She replied, 'Which one will win is difficult to say now. It all depends on the wolf that you decide to feed the most.'

Intellect brings order to our train of thoughts and actions. This order is called concentration. It is the power of concentration that separates a good learner from an average learner.

An Educator is More Than a Traffic Policeman

Think what a traffic policeman or a doctor does for a living. The traffic cop regulates the flow of chaotic traffic. The physician strives to bring your physical body to its orderly functioning. How do they do it? The traffic cop does it by mastering a consistent set of rules by which traffic moves, slows down and stops. The physician does it by measuring and regulating the vital signs of the body such as pulse rate, body temperature and respiratory rate. A traffic cop upholds the value of orderly traffic and a physician addresses the value of health.

The educator in a school regulates behaviour of students in and outside the class. This is just the outer aspect of the teacher's role. The real goal of the teacher is to bring about coherence of values that binds the school as a community. Three of the values that create learning communities are—commitment to truth, absence of fear and reverence for life and Nature.

Knowing Your Subjects

Lata Vaidyanathan, the principal of Modern School in Delhi talked about a Q&A session that Mahatma Gandhi had with teachers. Gandhi was asking them about the subjects they taught. The answers were predictably around the teacher's expertise. They responded by saying things like, 'I teach history', 'I take geography' and 'I am a mathematics teacher'. Gandhi turned around and asked this stunning question, 'Does anyone teach a student here?'

Here is another question that I can add here to amplify what Gandhi was asking:

What is more important to a teacher—the content of teaching or the brain state of the learner?

If downloading the content is all that matters, then teachers end up becoming content fillers like those gas station salesmen who fill cars with petrol.

A teacher's obsession with 'finishing' the teaching hours

makes learning a function of periods rather than the mental capacity of the learner. Some learners may take one period to learn the laws of thermodynamics while some others may take several. Students learn best, not when they are racing against time but when they are able to set their own pace and learn in their own way.

Good Teachers Explain; Great Teachers Enliven!

Professor Yash Pal is of one India's most iconic teachers. A doctorate in physics from MIT, he has been an institution builder and a great communicator of complex science subjects. He has demonstrated that science can be enlivened. If a student asked a good physics teacher what 'gravity' was; he would get an explanation that would be largely conceptual or mathematical. Here is how Professor Yash Pal would explain gravity to students:

He would draw a circle representing the circumference of the earth. Then he would draw pictures of tiny human figures standing around the circle. He would point to a human form on the top of the circle and say, 'He is standing upright right at the top. That is not so surprising. But look at this fellow standing upright at the bottom of the earth. Do you now know what gravity is all about?' The whole class is enlivened by the mystery that gravity is.

Great teaching is the ability to distinguish between what can and needs to be explained and what cannot be explained. The working of a computer needs to be explained as it is made by the human mind. But a butterfly need not always be explained. A butterfly has to be seen with the gleaming eyes of wonder as it is a natural expression of life and not of the mind.

Telescope Does Not Discover a New Star, We Do.

Technology is the new toy for educators. Everyone talks about it, very few really know how to use it and fewer still understand why they are using it. I was listening to Professor Richard Rowe, former dean of Harvard's Education School and CEO of Open Learning Exchange who said that technology was almost 'too popular' for his comfort. Very often, Rowe argued, technology should be the last in the list of priorities of educators. 'When you want to build a house, you don't start with a hammer. Rather you start with the knowledge of what kind of house you want to build,' he said.

Technology does not create learning just as a hammer does not make a house. Technology simplifies or amplifies our learning capacity. A microscope enables us to see the micro world. A telescope helps us see the macro world. It is not the microscope or telescope that sees. The two instruments are just accessories for our eyes. It is we who see through our human capacity of visual perception. Too much obsession with technology is like trying to design a house with a hammer in hand. A teacher who does not really understand how to use technology is like a blind man who is given the world's most powerful telescope to gaze at the skies. Technology is only a tool. In medical schools, symptoms can be fed part by part into a computer, but a doctor has to understand the disease in relation to the whole body. Without understanding the disease, merely recording symptoms would not help. Technology follows illumination and understanding and not the other way round.

Seeing Stars in Broad Daylight!

A teacher leads a bunch of students outside the classroom to an open courtyard. In broad daylight he asks his students to look up at the sky and see if they can spot some stars there.

All the students look up.

The teacher asks, 'Do you see stars there?'

'No,' the students shake their heads.

'Really, are there no stars there?'

'No,' comes the reply again.

'Think again. There are stars out there where you just looked. It is another matter that you cannot see them unless it's night.'

The students stand there stupefied.

'So, do you only see with the eyes?' the teacher explored.

'Yes,' answered one student.

'Suppose your eyes were looking at the clock, but your mind was lost in daydreaming, can you say you were really seeing the clock?'

'Not really' answered the student rather sheepishly.

'So, it is the mind behind the eyes that makes seeing possible, isn't it?' quizzed the teacher.

'Yes. Yes!' gushed the student.

'Now, suppose the mind was behind the eyes all right but it was wandering around like a naughty child, will the eyes be able to see properly?' he asked further, 'do you realise that it is your intellect, your buddhi, that holds the mind in place so that the eyes can see?'

'But I can't see the intellect. How do I know that it is holding my mind in one place?' a student questioned.

It was the teacher's turn to ask the clinching question now, 'You can't see the stars in broad daylight even though they are there for you to see, can you?' A great teacher can show you stars in broad daylight by honing your intellect or buddhi. The word buddhi comes from budh or understanding. Although you do not see the stars in broad daylight through your physical eyes, you learn to see them through the eye of the mind—through the understanding imparted by your buddhi.

Not a Q&A Session, Just a Q&Q Session

What if a class teacher conducted a question and question session rather than a question and answer session? A question is a perpetual quest. A question is like an adventure in an unknown forest. It puts the brain on an alert and learning mode.

A problem-solving method called root cause analysis gets to the bottom of a problem by asking repeated questions. Root causes are identified depending on the way in which the problem or event is defined. For example, while looking at a full length mirror you may ask, 'Why is my image altered sideways (my right hand is shown as my left hand and vice versa) and not top to bottom (my head does not show up near my feet and vice versa)?

'Does this happen because of the way light is reflected from the mirror to my eyes?

'If not, is it that the brain plays some kind of trick on my eyes?

'Why does my brain play this trick?

'Is it because it is easier for the brain to turn my body 180 degrees and interpret the signals received from the mirror than to turn it upside down?

'Is it therefore the brain's convenience rather than a trick of light?'

By the time you came to the last question you will realise the root cause of the sideways rather than top-down shift of your image in a mirror. This is because of the ease with which your brain has learnt to interpret a lateral shift rather than a vertical shift.

Students Define the Classroom, Not the Walls

The classroom does not make up a class in the same way that iron bars do not make a prison. The real classroom is what is happening inside the head of the students—in the way they think; the manner in which they perceive facts and the way they process their thoughts.

A teacher who dominates the class with her formal authority is unwittingly creating a prison where students have stopped thinking for themselves. In such a class, the walls are not made up of concrete and iron bars, but of neural structures in the brain. Students are conditioned by fear. They stop thinking on their own. My best teacher was someone who demonstrated the power of informality in managing a class. For him all discipline began with self-discipline. He would meticulously prepare for every class. He would take a few minutes to make eye contact with every student before he uttered a single word. It was as though he was visually hugging every student. It was impossible for a student not to be attentive to whatever he was teaching. He combined creativity and discipline so effortlessly.

Students are Hosts, Not Hostages

It is a hostage situation out there! Teachers as well as parents hold students hostages through their marks and remarks. The student as a hostage is held to ransom by an unthinking teacher. The abductor sometimes does not even realise that he is holding a young mind hostage. The parents of the student have already paid the fees in an elite school as a down payment for future benefits. The living, breathing present in which the student wants to live is mortgaged to a successful future.

How about this as an idea—teachers in schools ought to treat students as their hosts. Teachers can make a guest appearance as long as the hosts want them. The guests must learn to disappear when they overwhelm their hosts with their unwelcome presence. Interestingly enough, at IIM, all courses and faculty teaching these courses are evaluated by students. One insight emerges from these evaluations—students often judge a teacher's ability based on the teacher's likability. Simply put, if students like a teacher, they seem to like the course. This has serious implications for teachers who are just focused on broadcasting content rather than connecting with students. Just as a gracious guest treats a host with utmost care, teachers would do well to see themselves as caregivers for students they teach. There are several ways to tell students that a teacher cares—a gentle touch, a disarming smile, a kind comment, a listening ear, an honest feedback—all of these have the potential to transform the teacher-student relationship.

Should Knowledge Chase Students?

One of India's foremost novelists, RK Narayan was made a member of upper house of the Indian Parliament for a while. He urged the parliamentarians in his only speech in the Rajya Sabha to do something about decreasing the burden of the school bag.

'The school bag has become an inevitable burden for the child,' he said, 'I am now pleading for abolition of the school bag, as a national policy, by an ordinance if necessary.' He was upset when he looked at young boys and girls going to school laden with books which they could hardly carry. 'This burden did not improve their minds; it only made them hunchbacks,' he said.

In some of the best schools of India, school bags are not that worrisome anymore. What worries students today is knowledge that is now chasing them from within compact discs and digital junk from smart classes. An explosion of knowledge resource has happened through the internet and the digital media. Knowledge is chasing students like never before. Who is worrying about curiosity that drives students towards knowledge? We now need teachers who can pull students to the classroom rather than push them into it.

The Rise of Soft Power Within the Hard Walls of Higher Education

The face of educational leadership is changing in the twenty-first century. The new face is softer and less formal than it was in the previous centuries. I recently had the privilege of meeting three female presidents of major US universities—Drew Faust, the first woman president of Harvard University, Susan Hockfield, the first woman and the first life scientist to hold the position of president of MIT and our own Renu Khator, the first Indian American woman to become the chancellor and president of a major American school, the University of Houston.

The three prima donnas of higher education represent the soft power of informality. Drew Faust is a champion of liberal education. She says that in the global economic crisis, her focus belongs not on what we have lost, but on what we have as our human heritage. In Faust's view, human progress is not just about forward thinking innovation but also about backward integration with our age-old values. As we adapt to a rapidly changing world, Drew Faust's Harvard harks back to long traditions of liberal education and of humanistic inquiry. These traditions can generate both the self-scrutiny and self-understanding that lead through doubt to wisdom. 'It is not Harvard's job to make carpenters out of men but to make men out of carpenters,' I remind her of her once famous utterance in a speech. She nods in agreement. Like her counterpart across the river, MIT's president Susan Hockfield represents the new narrative of higher education. She integrates rather than dissects issues during her conversation with us. She decides through informal consultation rather than formal authority.

The new story of higher education is about the plasticity of knowledge that 'flows' seamlessly across rigid disciplines. For a long time, higher education has been classified into false and misleading categories—physical versus life sciences, arts versus engineering. When knowledge flows across disciplines I would like to call it 'flowledge'—knowledge that is free-flowing and fluid. 'Flowledge' has given birth to such emerging disciplines as biomechanics, nuclear medicine and conscious capitalism.

In a way, 'flowledge' represents the rise of the creative whole brain from the predominant left-brain structures that ruled academia. This domination had created strict hierarchies and given birth to rigid and often impermeable disciplines. The age of the whole brain will set right some of the asymmetries in our cortical hemispheres. Here, women who bring those soft cortical skills and big-picture perception of life to the job will triumph over lopsidedly analytical and data distracted left-brainers. Nurtured by this new leadership, higher education will mean more than just 'hire' education. The mantra of higher education will be more like what Harvard's Drew Faust would like to imagine—making humans out of carpenters.

I shall return to Renu Khator whom I met informally over dinner hosted by India's ambassador to the US and then again formally at a meeting with India's education minister in Washington DC. Renu said that she comes from a small UP town of Farrukhabad, 'I was only eighteen years old when I got married. I cried for ten days as I wanted to pursue higher education rather than marriage.' Her husband, Suresh Khator, who now serves as professor at the same university where Renu serves as chancellor, fulfilled her desire to learn and lead. 'So, you are your husband's boss in school. How do you handle that?' Renu responds with unstudied grace and humility, 'My husband often introduces me as someone who his boss's boss reports to. He made me what I am today. I am the product of his contribution. I am grateful to him for that.' Her story blueprints the rise of a first generation Indian immigrant from an obscure town in North India to hard-earned glory in North America. She embodies the coming of age of soft power of India inside the once insular corner office of white Anglo-Saxon male dominated American education.

The New Narrative of a Business School

Business as usual does not work anymore after the global economic crisis. Naturally, business school as usual will not work anymore either. Business schools of this century will need a new narrative—a new story.

The old story was about impressive buildings, rigid functional focus and high quality analytical minds pressed into the service of crafting a pipeline of case studies from the prolific business case production factories in North American schools. Much of that has to change now. The centre of gravity of business is now shifting from the Atlantic to the Pacific. So there is likely to be a reverse flow of knowledge from the emergent economic crucibles like China and India into the classrooms of North American and European schools. Most B-schools in Asia have invested a lot more money in real estate rather than in real hands-on research agenda. They now have to move from just building to institution building. This can happen through focused and context-specific research. In order to remain relevant, Asian B-schools will have to move from cosmetic modification of curriculum created in North America to a cultural transformation. It is like moving beyond just shifting the furniture in the classroom to creating a radically different kind of classroom. Business schools will have to help local businesses and civic society solve real and contextual problems of the region.

Take the typical problems of a low-cost and high-quality human resources economy such as India with respect to health, housing and clean water. How a business school approaches a solution to the problem of 800 million Indians' need for inexpensive, clean drinking water or affordable medication for viral fever would go a long way in making the school very relevant and contemporary. Effective solutions to the above problems can also be replicable for three billion of the world's population living below the poverty line in emerging economies. The issue here is about the business schools' need for creating the intellectual architecture that makes sense of real and context sensitive solution to problems that are often far away from the concerns of the Wall Street.

North American and West European schools will, in turn, have to look towards co-creation and co-production of knowledge with their Asian counterparts to remain globally relevant. Solutions based on logical-rational analysis, a gift of Western thought, will have to mingle with the intuitive, imaginative and storytelling mode of processing reality that is the legacy of Asian culture.

Business school students will have to contend increasingly

with issues of ethics and sustainability. Instead of myopic quarter-to-quarter thinking, they have to ask—what does a successful business look like five years from now?

What is that sustainable change process that will take me there? The businesses of the future will be certified more by the community and less by Wall Street or Dalal Street.

Finally, the world will see the emergence of movements such as conscious capitalism and managing through trusteeship led by organisations like Whole Foods in the US and the House of Tatas in India. Business schools of the future will have to rally behind the emerging need for a more inclusive and humane process of globalisation. In this growth, the very ethos of a B-school will need a serious makeover. In curriculum design, faculty development and in defining the very purpose of a business school, we have to abandon much of the narrow functional focus that we have been used to for several decades. Instead, we have to ponder over how all functional disciplines can come together in sustaining this fragile planetary system. Business schools of the future will have to view business success in the context of its larger ecosystem. They have to look beyond the blinkers set by exclusive stakeholder need for profiteering and crass opportunism.

Harvard Yogi

Harvard Business School is a place where you are supposed to know something about everything. Picture two adjacent lecture rooms. In Room 101 there is a conference on How To Know God and in Room 102 God Himself is the guest speaker. Where do you think the Harvard guys would queue up? You almost got it... they would queue up before 101 to know about God and leave God Himself alone in 102 to listen to his own lecture.

I met this man once in the middle of Harvard Square. He called himself Yogi and started chatting with a handful of business school students. He had long unruly hair like Albert Einstein's and a beard like Karl Marx's.

'Why do yogis grow such unnatural hair?' a student asked him in a condescending voice. Yogi shot back, 'Unnatural? You think this is unnatural? Isn't it perfectly natural for hair to grow? Isn't that the real dharma of all hair anywhere in the world? You guys trim, twist, tie, tonsure and inflict tattoos on your head and call that natural! What a lopsided way of educating yourself!'

Saying this, he sat cross-legged drinking French vanilla coffee. He put down his coffee mug and began his tirade against all that mumbo-jumbo they teach in executive education in the name of corporate social responsibility. Here is the gist of what he said in between sips, 'There is accounting and goal setting in the world of business, but no accounting for your own life. You are the CEO of your Life Corp. Is there a goal for Life Corp?' Then, he proceeded to answer his own question, 'The only goal of Life Corp is simply to live—just to live fully! To live fully is to taste undying bliss!' A woman in a ponytail asked, almost whispering as if to coax out a secret from him, 'What is then the way of getting this bliss?' Yogi replied rather matter-of-factly, 'Just when you drop this silly idea of getting bliss someplace else—bliss will crawl to you like your pet poodle.'

Yogi drew a deep breath, had another infusion of coffee and went on, 'You get travelling in exactly the opposite direction of the path that brings all the pleasures of life. You seek pleasure by moving away from yourself. You can get a Ferrari, fancy titles, a Barbie girlfriend, a fat pay packet and a slim body. However, you can't get bliss that way. All that you will get is a temporary bubble, a fleeting euphoria of the senses that froths up from an ocean of concealed bliss within yourself. Disappointed, you will pitch for the next getting. There comes a time in one's life when one arrives at this heartbreaking conclusion—I have got many things, but I have lived a poor life indeed.'

'Then?' asked a mid-career MBA student with a hint of sad desperation in his voice.

'Then you start the real search for bliss which is lodged deep inside you like fragrant musk that is lodged inside the navel of a musk deer. Like that poor deer, Harvard graduates run around the concrete jungles of business in the desperate search for this intoxicating fragrance called life. By the time they discover that this life had to be lived rather that "got", they are half dead.'

'But doesn't Harvard teach you a thing or two about managing this complex world of ours?' enquired the ponytailed woman.

Yogi smiled from ear to ear. 'That's what I thought when I came to teach at Harvard a long time ago.' Then he vanished, just as he had appeared, into the hazy Boston night with these parting words, 'Talk about managing the world, hey? For a hundred years and more the enlightened Harvard gurus haven't been able to manage their own parking space problems on campus.'

Not Multiple Intelligence. Just One Unified Intelligence Wearing Multiple Masks

A prominent milestone in the twenty-first century education mission is the Theory of Multiple Intelligence. This theory is attributed to Howard Gardner, a very eminent professor of education at Harvard University. In simple language, this theory advocates that human beings have different kinds of intelligence such as linguistic (aptitude for language and words) and spatial intelligence (learning through visual images). Gardner argues that the surest route to mind changing in the classroom then, is the effective exploitation of multiple intelligences. According to Gardner, if a learner is exposed to multiple modes of instruction such as through books, pictures, audio tapes and puzzles, the learner's mind is likely to change based on the kind of intelligence he or she specialises in.

Our greatest teachers, the seers, have taught us, however,

that our universe has only one kind of intelligence. It is the intelligence of the whole. Every other form of intelligence is like the whole wearing a mask to disguise itself. The intelligence of the whole keeps our planets in the orbit and our bones rightly aligned so that we can walk around without difficulty. Imagine if one bone formation, the skull, declared independence and decided to outgrow other bones by specialising in its activity. The result will be a swollen head and perhaps an ungainly horn on your head that would make your social life quite miserable.

By fragmenting intelligence in multiple categories, as Gardner does, how can teachers enhance a student's comprehension of the wholeness of intelligence. Can one understand a living human being by dissecting the parts of a dead body in a medical school? Can criminal law be taught separately from sociology of crime in a law school? Can business management be taught without reference to environmental contexts in which a manager lives and works?

A teacher's most important work is to be able to connect the part to the whole. In this endeavour, he has to look beyond multiple intelligences to unified intelligence. A teacher can look at a rose and simultaneously show students a delicate architecture in the arrangement of its petals; the chemical properties of its fragrance or evoke in the learner the aesthetic appreciation of the rose. A spider's web can be, at the same time, a feat of civil engineering and a work of art. If a teacher were to look at a single spider and study it's intelligence in isolation, she would discover very little evidence of intelligence. However, when a single spider is connected to the intelligence of its whole environment, something as stunningly functional as a spider's web becomes possible. At IIM Kozhikode, thirty-two of my faculty team members taught a course that was titled 'Perspectives'. This course made an attempt to see the world of business through the lenses of finance, marketing, organisation behaviour and other disciplines. The learning experience for students was like climbing a mountain top through multiple slopes. Each slope was like a different discipline that ultimately led to the same peak of learning.

Serious Form of Education—
Dropping Out of School

For them, dropping out of school meant dropping into the rest of the universe that had no formal curriculum. A life without school does not mean that Rabindranath Tagore and Bill Gates had a life without teachers. Our teachers are everywhere. Every human being can be a potential teacher. Every creature in Nature is a teacher. Many of the yoga postures of India were based on the yogis' observation of animals and birds. They discovered the crocodile posture, the fish posture, the snake posture and even the corpse posture by observation.

A school that standardises learning also limits the horizon of learning in many ways. Someone once asked a school teacher whether tomato was a fruit or a vegetable. The teacher searched the internet for an either/or answer. After a thorough search, he came to the conclusion that tomato is a fruit by definition 'and' a vegetable by way of consumption. School dropouts such as Gates or Tagore are not always tied up in an either/or universe. They drop into a universe of 'and'. The universe of 'and' is not one of narrow horizons, but of broad possibilities.

No Mind, Beautiful Mind!

The ordinary mind is a mob. It is an unruly march of thoughts that have no real connection with each other. I have been watching my mind ever since I can remember. It is one of the most fascinating and perhaps the most rewarding occupation that I can recommend.

For one thing, our perception of the world is manufactured in the factory of mind. When we see a beautiful mountain peak and point our finger towards what we see, we certainly point in the wrong direction. The mountain peak is experienced nowhere else but in those specialised centres in the brain such as the visual cortex.

Most of our educators are obsessed with teaching from the text. Yet, teachers rarely realise that nothing has been taught unless it is learnt. Learning rarely happens through a text. Real learning happens in context. Take the case of a geography teacher who is teaching geography from a text. She can end up teaching about the soil quality and the temperature required for growing rice in certain regions of the world. Her students will tend to mechanically memorise data about the optimum temperature to grow rice. They will also download this data on the answer paper of the examination. However, they would have had no real learning about the context in which rice is grown.

Instead, if the same teacher was to expose the students to a real paddy field, their minds will register a tactile appreciation of the soil where paddy is cultivated. They will have a direct perception of the textures and temperatures; the colours and the context in which paddy flourishes. When the learner is young, he experiences much of the world through the senses rather than through verbal and numerical symbols. Learning geography in such a manner will help the students enter into a deep communion with their subject. They are also likely to have a compassionate and nurturing relationship with their own environments.

A mind that is cut off from the touch and feel of our universe simply learns to manipulate the universe through words and symbols. It can calculate the distance between Earth and Mars without having to travel in space. This is indirect and approximate knowledge. Such knowledge is proximate but not real. Have you wondered what it would be like to actually travel to Mars?

When we start watching our mind, we realise that it is full of neural noise. This kind of noise emanates from the relentless buzz of thoughts that often have nothing to do with our reality. Yet, strangely, this noise tends to subside as we begin to watch our thoughts. There comes a time when the mind can be completely empty of thoughts like a clear sky without a single cloud. Such a state can also arise in a state of extreme ecstasy or grave danger when our lives are threatened. A mind emptied of all its content becomes a no-mind. No-mind is not dull mindlessness. No-mind is agile and electric. A no-mind can see reality directly without the screen of conditioned thoughts.

The no-mind is also a beautiful mind. It can receive the first impressions of the world out there without psychological distortion. Like a child stands enraptured watching a feather fall in a gentle gliding motion, the no-mind can discover beauty in the most mundane events around us. A thoughtful mind keeps on exploring the essence of reality that the no-mind finally discovers. This discovery has the enchantment of homecoming that the English poet TS Eliot describes so well in *Little Gidding*:

We shall not cease from exploration
And the end of all our exploring
Will be to arrive where we started
And know the place for the first time

Better Children for Our Planet

I invited an education evangelist, Aarti Rajaratnam to my Leading Schools class. This class brings together talented teachers from many leading schools around the world. Aarti runs self-help groups that she calls Prosperity Rings. These 'rings' provide day care and education for economically deprived children in Indian villages. The communities that her work embraces include children of tsunami victims, migrant labourers and even gypsies. She sometimes transforms an abandoned van into a makeshift classroom.

Aarti feels that it does not cost much to bring back these marginalised children to school. She likes to describe herself as a twenty-first century Robin Hood, asking the rich among Indians to pay for the economically impoverished children. There was one thing that struck me as remarkable in Aarti's speech that day, 'It is time we had better children for our planet than look for a better planet for our children.'

Just think of it. Our planet is nothing but a man-made disaster waiting to happen. Global warming, excessive flooding, alarming levels of pollutants in air, water and earth—all of these and more are the results of generations of human beings that have collectively depleted this planet. In addition to trying to fix the planet, we must work on the minds and hearts of a new generation of children who will not add to the crisis that generations before them have brought about.

A teacher creates a new generation. A school can be a space for generative ideas. One idea of mine that has inspired my institution is our vision for 2047. That year will be the fiftieth anniversary of IIM Kozhikode and hundredth year of independent India. Our students and faculty have begun to think what our planet, our country and our school will look like in 2047. We realised that around that time, India will move ahead of China as the most populous country in the world with a projected population of 1.6 billion people. The Indian economy will easily be among the top three largest economies of the world. If one human being is considered the unit of currency of a nation rather than a dollar, a renminbi or a rupee, then India will find itself as the richest nation of the world by virtue of its human potential. India's voice in the coming years will be of planetary proportion. As a school, this one idea made us feel more responsible as citizens of a great country.

Qualified Teachers are Not Always Quality Teachers

There are plenty of qualified teachers. But quality teachers are so rare! Teaching is a craft, rather than a qualification. Learning to be a quality teacher is like learning to make vintage wine. Both require time and years of culture. I served as an apprentice to a great teacher who asked me to just sit in his class and listen. Just listen for two years! Each time I would want to utter a word, he would signal me to keep quiet. Listening, though somewhat forced like a bottle of wine locked up in a cellar, ultimately helped in my maturation as a teacher.

When teachers are not happy being teachers, it becomes a real problem. More often than not, they are forced to take up the profession because it provides the security of a 'job'. After acquiring a degree in education, many teachers get into a groove of subject teaching. They start teaching for tests. Their minds and hearts harden prematurely without the inner maturity that comes with self-awareness. Qualified teachers who lack those qualities of head and heart such as authenticity and empathy for students are like teaching machines. They churn out an assembly line of students for the competitive world outside. In the process, what the world gets is mostly unthinking, ruthless and corrupt men and women who lead our societies.

Quality teachers evolve through constant practice of their craft and diligent self-reflection. If they are lucky, they get inspiring mentors who give them valuable feedback and insights into their own strengths and vulnerabilities. I have heard that it takes a person no less than ten thousand hours of practice to achieve mastery over any craft. That would mean three to four hours of practice every day for ten years at a stretch. Teachers can spend those ten thousand hours repeating the same lessons over and over again till the cows come home. Alternatively, they can reflect on how they teach, and learn from their own mistakes. This way they can eventually master the craft of teaching.

3 Idiots and a Thankless Profession

I had gone to watch this Hindi movie called *3 Idiots* that had caused quite a stir in a nation where wise men and idiots flourish in equal measure. I felt like the fourth idiot sitting through some marvellous trashing of the teaching profession. Shot largely in a location in the IIM Bangalore campus, *3 Idiots* was ironically messaging exactly what IIMs and IITs ought not to be doing. The film's protagonist Aamir Khan had actually spent days in a hostel room in the IIM to 'get used' to life in an institution of professional excellence. In brief, the movie's message could be summarised in four short and idiot proof sentences:

1. Educational institutions are like police lock-ups
2. The principals/directors of schools are prison superintendents.
3. Teachers are certified idiots.
4. The real prisoner is excellence that is latent in every talented student.

Naturally, it required Aamir Khan, a school dropout turned Bollywood icon, to suggest ways and means of transforming the whole education system in under three hours—the equivalent of four contact classes in a school. What did he suggest? Make fun of your teachers. They are just incapable, impractical book worms, anyway. Loyalty to a friend comes before law. Steal question papers to help a friend pass those ridiculous exams. Delve into your prodigious talent to top the merit list without ever referring to books. Then, retire happily ever after in your private island with multiple patents against your name with a girlfriend perpetually wearing a helmet to keep you company. Truly and deliciously idiotic! Predictably, the whole nation lapped it up. There was talk of the movie going to the Oscars! Save my soul!

The movie kept me wondering what I was doing in the teaching profession that was as thankless a job as scratching a rhino's back. *3 Idiots* points fingers at all that is wrong with our education system. The hapless director cum the seemingly ruthless professor of the school, who was far from ideal, is not a standalone villain that this movie makes him out to be. He is just a cog in the large wheel of the factory model of education. In this model, students are 'products' mass manufactured for the consumption market. The real villain is the inhuman process that makes education a slave of the market. Yet, the market can only differentiate the efficient from the inefficient, it cannot differentiate between good and bad. It is only wisdom and not market logic that can decide what is good and what is bad and how they are interrelated.

In *3 Idiots*, the good and the bad seem as separate as chalk and cheese. Yet, in our human universe, goodness is not the opposite of the bad. True goodness sees the bad not as a demon but as goodness obscured—as a victim of a much bigger process of cause and effect. Think of Ravana in the *Ramayana*, the ultimate villain, who dies with the name of Rama on his lips and is happy that his death happens at the hands of a good man. In fact, bad is like the darkest hour before dawn—that phase before the light of goodness is about to break out. *3 Idiots* is a good film but not good enough to tell us the whole truth about our education system. What I feel really does is this story I received from a friend in mail. It made my day and I thought this was truly worth sharing:

The dinner guests were sitting around the table generally discussing life.

One man, a CEO (proud of being a professional) decided to explain the problem with the education system. He argued, 'What's a kid going to learn from someone who decided his best option in life was to become a teacher?'

He reminded the other dinner guests what they say about teachers, 'Those who can, do. Those who can't, teach...'

To stress his point he said to another guest, 'You're a teacher, Shobha. Be honest. What do you make?'

Shobha, who had a reputation for honesty and frankness replied, 'You want to know what I make?'

She paused for a second, then began, 'Well, I make kids work harder than they ever thought they could.

'I make a C+ feel like the Olympic Bronze medal.

'I make kids sit through forty-five minutes of class time when their parents can't make them sit for five minutes without an iPod, Game Cube or movie rental.

'You want to know what I make?' She paused again and looked at each and every person at the table.

'I make kids wonder.

'I make them question.

'I make them apologise and mean it.

'I make them have respect and take responsibility for their actions.

'I teach them to write and then I make them write. Keyboarding isn't everything.

'I make them read, read, read.

'I make them show all their work in math. They use their God given brain, not the man-made calculator.

'I make my students from other countries learn everything they need to know in English while preserving their unique cultural identity.

'I make my classroom a place where all my students feel safe.

'Finally, I make them understand that if they use the gifts they were given, work hard and follow their hearts, they can succeed in life.'

Shobha paused one last time and then continued, 'Then, when people try to judge me by what I make, with me knowing money isn't everything, I can hold my head up high and pay no attention because they are ignorant...You want to know what I make? I make a difference. What do you make Mr CEO?'

His jaw dropped, he went silent.

Compassion is Action

The typical educator of today is an unhappy person. She is unhappy about loss of control over students. She is unhappy about CCE (Continuous and Comprehensive Evaluation)—many interpret this as Complete Confusion in Education. She is unhappy about parental negligence of children. She is unhappy about unsympathetic and competitive co-workers. She is unhappy about her powerlessness in the face of ruthless authorities whether it is the board or the government. She is unhappy about having to take on macroscopic responsibility with microscopic salaries. Unhappiness is not an educator's natural condition. It is a learnt behaviour.

How does an educator learn to be unhappy? First, she sets herself up for unhappiness in the way she defines success. She has been influenced by the market society's strange invention that defines success as consumption and acquisition of experience. In the market economy, you are what you consume.

Your status as a nation or as an individual is defined in terms of GDP or per capita income. The desire for more consumption evoked by mass media translates as the will to consume. In a resource constrained earth, the will to consume of one individual dominates the will to consume of others. This sets in motion waves of envy and competitive frenzy. The market out there is nothing but a superstructure that is projected on a shared ethos of pitiless competition and unviable consumption.

When the situation is such, what does an educator really do as a member of such a society? How does she get out of the grind of everyday experience that does not really fulfil her? The only way out of the treadmill of consumption is a life of creation. A life of creation starts with a wider definition of success. When success is defined in terms of exclusive personal possession, one will always remain insecure about losing what one has. Insecurity breeds fear. Exclusivity is the breeding ground of fear. When the educator actually sees this, she will think of success that will include others. This will make the educator more compassionate. Compassion is action. They are not two separate things. I will tell a story that will put this in proper perspective. I had this teacher who had a desire to own a farmhouse before turning thirty. One day, on the verge of retirement, he announced, 'Finally I have become a farmhouse owner!'

'Really?' asked his amused colleagues, tongue-in-cheek.

The euphoric teacher proceeded to explain, 'One of my favourite students has become hugely successful with his start-up company. He has just bought an exotic farmhouse near my city. He just called in to say that I could live in his farmhouse as long as I was alive. Imagine! He is just twenty-nine. Don't you think WE have made it?'

We need to connect with the source and not just be a resource. A source is generative like the seed of a tree. You can create a forest of a million trees from that one seed. Yet this will still not exhaust the generative power of that seed. A resource is like a branch of a tree. If you chop off that branch from its source, the branch will not be able to regenerate itself.

If Livelihood is for Life, What is Life for?

Teaching leadership is simple. Only students have become more complicated. All they want from me is an exotic formula to describe their own passion. I would like to say that leadership is what I attempt to teach when I am not speaking. Honestly, leadership can't be taught, it can only be discovered. Like you can't teach anyone how to love; you can only teach them dating protocols—they fall or rise in love by themselves!

I had this student in the IIM class of 2003 whose name was Manjunath. He was not our typical business school whiz kid who had a head for cold 'sadistics' (sad about statistics) or 'maniac' (management accounting) or 'biogas' (behaviour in organisation) classes. He would warm up to anything that aroused his passion. He loved to sing and he loved to lead. He was like this bird of the wilderness that sang, not to win a musical competition, but because he had discovered a freedom song inside his own heart.

In a business school, the job you get at the end of the placement process determines your worth in your peer group. Manjunath found himself in an unglamorous location in Lakhimpur-Kheri in western Uttar Pradesh, supervising distribution of petrol and diesel in several filling stations on behalf of the Indian Oil Corporation. Unlike his classmates who had cushy marketing jobs in multinationals, Manjunath had a very modest beginning. But he took his work rather seriously.

Business school academics was not really Manjunath's cup of tea. He would often come to me to discuss questions that were not about personal success or career. He would raise questions about the meaning of life itself. He was like a wild eagle looking beyond its nest for an adventure in the wilderness. 'If livelihood is for life, what is life for?' I asked Manjunath when he was visiting his teachers at his alma mater, IIM, Lucknow. This time, it was a one-on-one class between the two of us about life in general and professional life in particular. He didn't have an answer to my question.

A month later, on a dark November night in 2005, Manjunath was shot dead by the oil mafia in Uttar Pradesh. His crime—he had sealed three petrol pumps that were selling adulterated fuel. Manjunath died honestly doing his job; defending the cheated Indian customer. Is that the end of the story? No, not quite. As the news of Manjunath's brutal killing reached some of us, I called up the editors of two of the most respected newspapers of India. I sent frantic mails to whoever I could. One mail I sent out read:

'We shall not let Manjunath vanish quietly into the night. We shall not give in to fear and murder without a fight.'

The whole nation responded. I received phone calls from shocked politicians and bureaucrats. A mother who had lost her young son to the mafia called in offering help.

Manjunath made headlines posthumously on the national media. He even showed up as a potential Indian of the year. He had outdone his classmates because of what he died for. I was not his teacher anymore. Honestly, he became my teacher. The day before he was killed, Manjunath sang to his mother. He will sing no more. Yet, why does his voice still ring in my ears, 'Sir, what is this life if we have nothing to die for?'

Life is a Succession of Living Forms

Every new leaf is like a new born child—it is a promise. Soon the leaf will mature, flutter a few days in the breeze, then wear out and die. Life will be lived through us in a succession of living forms.

LEARN.
TEACH.
BE.

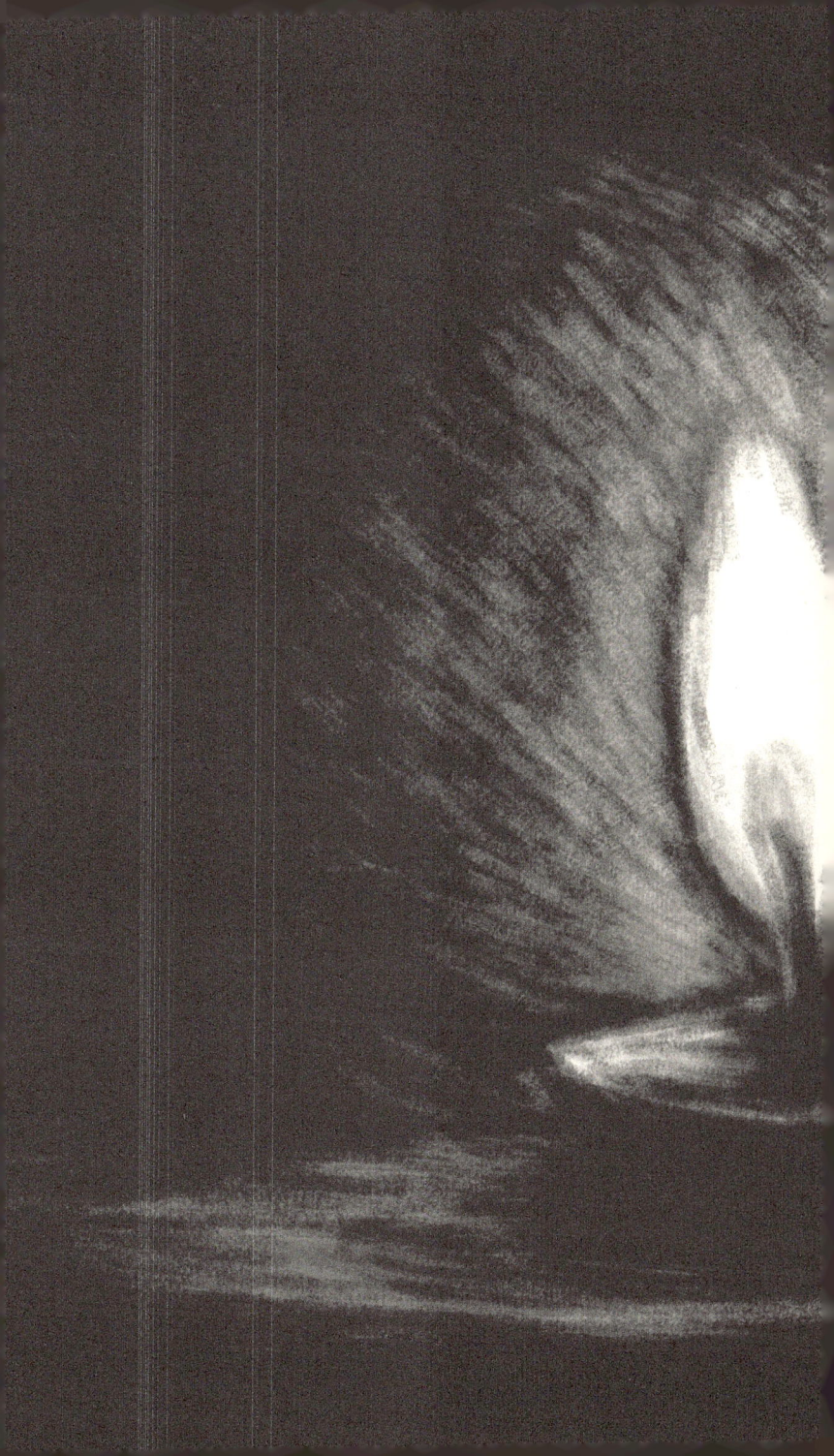

Very often as kids
GROW UP,
parents stop growing with them. They just
GROW OLD.

We Are Born Liars

Yes, you heard me right. We are born liars. Alright, if you want me to be more diplomatic, we are born storytellers. The fact that we lie or spin stories at will is not the point. The important thing is that the most lies we tell are to ourselves and about ourselves. The worst part is that we do not even realise that we are telling those lies to ourselves. I often ask two questions to people I coach:

1. Where are you?
2. Who are you?

The answer to the first question is, more often than not, about a physical place, 'I am at home in my study room.' That's a lie. Or at best, pure fiction. The person concerned is never fully present in the study room although her body is located there. Her mind has wandered off to some other place. The second question fetches such usual response as 'My name is...' or, 'I am so and so'. That's another set of stories. My name tells us as much about who I am as the name UFO tells us about an Unidentified Flying Object. Just think of this—all your descriptions of yourself are simply different names you give to the same human being that you are. You can take a glass of water and add some drops of lemon to it and call it lemonade. Alternatively, you can dip a bag of tea in the same water and call it Darjeeling tea. In essence, all you get are different flavours of the same water. Similarly, your name and the various roles you play are only like the many flavours of the same Self that is you. Once you are rooted in the conviction that you are essentially the same Self assuming different roles, a lot of problems of life get sorted out. A large number of problems in our lives happen because we forget who we really are and get deluded by who we are not. For instance, a policeman is just a man playing the role of the police. If the same policeman takes up a job as a manager he remains the same man in a different role. The ability to separate the role from the Self is indeed a rare ability.

To know and to be quietly aware that we are not who we assume ourselves to be and that we are not where we say we are—is the beginning of the journey of an authentic life. The rishis of India described the journey of human life in terms of four destinations or *purushartha*s. The word *purusha* refers to the unmanifest source of life. You can describe *purusha* as the body you had before your parents were born. The *purusha* is our original being. *Purusha* is the ultimate ancestor of all our ancestors. Like the way invisible white light becomes a spectrum of seven colours when it is intercepted by objects, the *purusha* moves towards four destinations when it manifests in the human form. The four *purusharthas* represent the journey of the pure and invisible light of consciousness through four facets of life. These four facets that are like the primary colours of the consciousness are (i) Dharma (the truth of our being), (ii) Artha (our being in pursuit of its own abundance), (iii) Kama (the desire that arises when we crave something outside of ourselves and are therefore distanced from our being) and (iv) Moksha (the end of desire when the being finally reclaims itself).

The journey of our life through these four destinations can be described as the journey of a man who is standing on one bank of a river in full flow. He wants to cross over to the other side of the river. In order to do this he has to learn to negotiate the flowing, abundant and treacherous river that presents him with threats (drowning) as well as opportunities (swimming with the tide). The two banks of the river represent dharma and moksha—truth and freedom. While the river in between is artha and kama (abundance and desire). The rishis of India describe the destination of life as 'getting to the other side'. In reality this is a metaphor for reclaiming the safe ground of the original being by wading through the currents of desire and abundance.

In another sense, the flowing river is nothing but our ever desiring, forever fluctuating mind that takes us away from our own being, our most secure base, from us. The destination of life is nothing more than the mastery of this river-like mind.

When we tell ourselves that we are in a certain place out in the world, we tell only half the truth. That certain place is not a place at all, it is a mental state. Even our physical body is nothing more than an accumulation of sensory experiences that are located in the mind. We are forever situated in our mental world. When this mental world becomes calm like a river without ripples, our world appears calm. When the mental world is turbulent, our world too becomes turbulent. The way to cross this mental chasm is to act from our dharma—the truth of our being—even when we pursue desire or wealth. Our rishis have the last word when they describe pleasure without conscience and wealth without morality as sure ways to miss one's final destination—the other bank of moksha or freedom. They describe moksha as pure and free—being 'un-clutched' from the crosscurrents of the mind.

Basic Instinct

Our basic instinct is something that is innate to us. It is not something we pursue or learn. A bird does not learn to sing. A bird is instinctively 'songful'. Similarly a human being does not have to learn to be joyful. We are instinctively joyful. The reason we do not experience joy is that we have learnt its exact opposite—to be sorrowful. Sorrow is mental suffering or pain caused by injury, loss or despair. While pain is physical, sorrow and misery are mental states. Sometimes pain cannot be avoided, however, sorrow can be unlearnt. This is simply because sorrow is not real, sorrow is a mental make-up.

While joyfulness is the soft core of our existence, sorrow is the mental organisation around the soft core, like the hardened shell of a coconut. Joylessness is a learnt behaviour. Whenever we access the source of joy inside us, we get organised outward to capture it. The moment we see a sunset, we whip out a camera. We see a tender flower, we are itching to pluck it and put it inside a vase. What we do not realise is that the charm of the sunset or the beauty of the flower can be felt inside the soft core of our joyful self, it can't be felt by the lens of the camera or the inert vase.

Our current way of living has organised us away from the source of joy inside. It has misled us into believing that joy can be captured by drawing our senses outside through crafty contraptions. The world of advertisement promises a lot of joy in the latest 3D television or the latest car model. It is true that great advertisements really evoke our quest for joy, but they take us to those places where we can never really find it. The car or the TV is valuable but that's not where we can find what we really value—the innate core of joy residing within us.

Pursuit of joy outside of us is as futile as the pursuit of our own shadow. Our shadow recedes from us even as we pursue it. My own experience is that joy results as we retreat to the core of who we are. Like the Atlantic salmon, we have to swim upstream against the outbound current of our senses to find joy. Salmons will return from the sea to spawn in the same fresh water rivers and streams where they were once hatched. Sometimes they are known to retreat up to a thousand miles upstream to their original birthplace. Likewise, we have to earn joy swimming against the tide of our outbound senses.

You are Not Hardwired to be Angry or Fearful, Your Brain is

In the middle of a talk for corporate coaches, who had gathered in Bengaluru from several countries, I faced a question. The question may sound familiar to many readers of this book. This coach was saying, 'I am hardwired to be angry. I reach a flashpoint of anger very soon if my students are not following my instructions. How do I change that?'

I reflected on that question and said, 'You are not hardwired. Your brain is.' There was a 'learningful' silence in the room. I added, 'You have a brain, you are not your brain. This is almost like saying that you have a computer; you are not your computer. Just as you have hardwired your brain, you can also rewire your brain.'

I gave him examples of several students I met who could make voluntary changes in some of their well entrenched thinking and behavioural patterns. One of them gave up a smoking habit of ten years. Yet another student who was a compulsive latecomer in class learnt to be punctual. Finally, I shared notes on a student of mine named Gaurav, who trained his brain in such a way that his body could go through severe winters even in the Himalayan regions of north India with nothing more on him than a flimsy cotton attire.

They had defied their hardwired brains through a simple but demanding process. They just observed the content of their thoughts, emotions and behaviours on a daily basis. This observation was without judgement or without any immediate need to change anything about their behaviour. As observation became more objective and dispassionate, more the patterns of toxic thinking and toxic behaviour began to change. In short, they started directing the brain rather than letting the brain direct them. One of my successful experiments in the teaching profession was to get my students to enhance their focus on their own thoughts during examination. From years of experience, we know how stressed students can get before taking an important test. Sometimes they get quite panicky. While setting my test paper I would put a condition for all the test takers. They were not allowed to write or put pen to paper in the first fifteen minutes of a three hour test. All that they could do was to observe their own thought processes and patterns of emotions that arose as they prioritised their options of attempting the test. As students sharpened their observation of their own thoughts and emotions, they gained greater composure. Eventually they reported that the sacrifice of those fifteen minutes actually enhanced their test taking ability.

Darshan = Sight+Insight

The Greek notion of practical intelligence comes from a certain depth of insight conveyed by the Sanskrit word *darshan*. Practical intelligence is a function of integral vision, the ability to integrate sight and insight. *Darshan* is the awareness of the depth and magnificence of the moment. When we pay total attention to the reality of the moment, we become one with the moment. The wall between us and reality comes down. We become the reality itself. A great degree of energy is released as a result of our participation in reality. Personal mastery is the embodiment of the energy released by this participation. The great Greek philosopher Archimedes called this energy Eureka, which signified the great excitement and wonder of a new discovery.

Imagination Designs the Future. Reason Decodes It

I spent a while visiting Harvard Business School this summer. It was a time for alumni reunion. The crimson campus across river Charles was wrapped in a haze of nostalgia. The class of 1998 walked hand in hand with the class of 2020. The mother was now an eminent investment banker and her little daughter, holding her hand, was looking gleefully at a passing squirrel. She hardly knew that her mother was dreaming up a gorgeous future for her on this very campus where she had first struck fortune. She introduced her daughter to me saying, 'Our future is here.' 'Not so,' I said, pointing back towards her, 'You are her future. What you do today shapes your daughter's identity, for better or for worse.' That set her thinking.

'How many teeth does a squirrel have?' I asked her daughter who was still eyeing a squirrel that was nibbling away at a huge popcorn with its tiny mouth. Without moving her eyes, the kid urged, 'Bring me that squirrel, I will count and tell you how many teeth it has.' I turned to her mother and said, 'A die hard pragmatist—Harvard material, your daughter!' We laughed like most adults who do not understand children too well. Yet, I realised that what I had said was more in earnest than in jest.

If we are the future of our children, then it seemed to me, that future was very uncertain. First, the future no longer was going to be governed entirely by engineers, accountants and lawyers. Those professions that are dominated by predictable structures, numbers and rules will be gobbled up by computers with genie like powers of data processing. Second, the future itself would be so predictably unpredictable that one will always be ready to face a future that will no longer happen. We will behave like an eighty-year-old man with wrinkles who looks at a mirror and sighs, 'They don't make good mirrors these days'. Third, we will have to analyse the past a lot less and imagine the future a lot more.

The future of education will belong to what Disney called 'imagineers'. Imagination and engineering are not two different functions. In Nature, there is no division between sophisticated engineering and spellbinding imagination. It requires much imagination and as much investigation to figure out how a black cow chewing green grass is able to produce white milk.

The future of education will have to do as much with law as with lyric. Mathematics and magic will have to coexist as 'mathemagic'. Learning will not just be about earning and acquisition—it will be about discovery. Teachers have to pass onto students the art of breaking free—liberating the energy of body and mind from mechanised, patterned, repetitive behaviours of computerised robots. Education has to bring back the lost reverence for life.

The world of education, as our Harvard mom would recognise, consists of a systems world and the human world.

The systems world of rules, laws, careers and curricula is made up of tried and tested answers. The human world of passion, poetry and prayer is made out of questions. The world of the future will be an exquisite synthesis of logic and lyric; the ascetic and the aesthetic. It will be more like multiple choice questions rather than one answer that is ticked inside a bubble. That bubble has long burst with the onset of the internet and the falling of the Berlin wall—roughly at the same turning point in our history. Like that little Harvard kid, we have to reimagine a world free of superstitions of science as well as religion.

As I reflected on this, that little child got curious about a black cat crossing our path near Baker Library. She asked me, 'What does a black cat crossing your path mean in India?' I looked into her green and hopeful eyes and said, 'It just means that the cat is going somewhere.' Who said that our children are our future? We ought to be their future.

Growing Up As a Father

I was born as a father on 4 April 1995 when Shrishti, whom I call 'my princess', appeared in my world. She dazzled my eyes with an exquisite charm and innocence that I never realised was a part of my being. The experience was not so much about 'having' a daughter as it was about 'becoming' a father! I was initiated by my princess from a world of romantic longing to a world of belonging.

Shortly after her birth, I had to leave for the United States for a ten-month academic exile in Minnesota. When we reunited at the Kolkata airport, after what seemed like eternity, my little bewitching princess had turned into a shy child. After the initial hesitation, she leapt on to daddy's lap. Finally, when we made eye contact, it was difficult to say who was watching and who was being watched. Years rolled on as the teenager became a 'screenager'—her lovely eyes would be glued to the television soaps more often than they would look for her daddy. We had our wars and we made peace. While she turned fifteen, here is what she wrote to me on email:

Dear Dad,

I see the purple shirt hanging neglected, the guitar that sleeps in its dusty cover, and I remember the times when these things had given me so much happiness. I brush my silver Vaio laptop and try to see the love that my father gave it to me with. He scolds me, screams at me, but at the end of the day these things remind me just how much he loves me. My Cinderella castle, that he brought home when I was six, speaks for itself. It whispers from the top of my desk that I'm truly the luckiest princess in the world. I know how much he loves me yet I cannot convince my teenage self. I love him too, I wait for him to come back every time he goes on his tours, I try to watch shows on BBC to show him that I take his advice seriously. I even agree with him on how 'breathtaking' our hills are although I can never appreciate its beauty like he does. When he talks of old memories, I wonder why he isn't that fond of me now, why is that baby me incomparable? I snap back, I'm rude, I'm rebellious, but am I not the example of a perfect teenager, so why can't he understand?

I don't want our relationship to be that bitter anymore. I just want us to be best friends. I have so many emotions running through me, so many secrets to share, I want us to have the best father–daughter relationship. I know just how much he loves me, and I'm sure somewhere even he knows that I love him deeply. If it's that simple, why can't we just show it!

I could sense through the mist that clouded my eyes and my mind that I had not grown up as well as a father as my princess had as a daughter. Here is what I scribbled to her as I hurried to catch the next flight:

My Princess,

First, I really enjoyed that writing—it's the best prose I have read in a long time—and it's no secret to you that I read a lot. I dream that my princess will one day become an inspiration for many. However, all dreams must go through a reality check before they come true. All the anger, resentment and criticism are the visible surface of a reality check...but they hide the deeper truth—dreams and aspirations of a father for his princess.

Like love, dreams cannot be shown—they will reveal themselves if and when they survive reality checks. These checks are like those parental sermons through which dreams are made real.

If I have wronged in saying things to my princess that should not have been said, I can easily say, 'Sorry, I did not mean to.' But, like I read in a book, love means never having to say you're sorry...because you trust each other enough to understand the real person behind the rude behaviour. Yes, it is that simple! This is not easy princess...even if it is simple...love you anyway!

They Come Through You but Not From You

The Scene:

Living room of an upper middle class Indian family. The father who controls the remote of a 32 inch television set is looking with an air of utter disgust at his thirteen-year-old. The teenager is lying on his back on a sprawling sofa glued to the latest video game. Here is how the conversation goes between father and son:

Father (watching a toilet soap commercial, howls in the direction of the teenager): Will you stop playing that video game?

Son (seeming completely indifferent to his father's howling, thinks inside his head): Is that old man from Neptune or something?

Father (screaming loudly): Will you STOP playing that video game?

Son (with ice cold eyes looking at his father): Tell me what I should do instead?

The son sulks and retreats to his study, banging the door behind him wishing it wasn't just the door he was banging.

The father continues to watch the television assuming that he has succeeded in getting his son to get off that video screen. The son, of course, knows better. He is not going to change his habit of playing that game eight hours a day; he will just get better at hiding from his father that he is playing his video game.

You can see why parental paranoia does not really help in bringing up well groomed children. Paranoia is a kind of madness—a delusional belief that parents can control children. The past generation in our country believed that learning had to be accompanied with pain and punishment. A whole generation of teachers made the cane as indispensable as a piece of chalk as tools of learning. That generation did not realise that delight or ananda was as much essential for learning as discipline was.

A former dean of Harvard University shared with me a real story about his daughter. He once looked at one of the English essays written by his daughter in standard IV. The English teacher wrote the word 'Excellent' on the margin of the essay. On closer examination, he found that she had made several grammatical mistakes in the essay that the teacher had apparently ignored. When he confronted his daughter's class teacher about why she wrote the 'Excellent' on what evidently was a work full of errors, this is what the class teacher had to say:

'Your daughter needs to love the English language more than she needs to know the exact rules of grammar. If I point out all her mistakes and rob her of her love for the subject, she will never learn English well. She can pick up the rules later in life, but she can never regain the love for her subject once she has lost it.'

Long ago, a Lebanese poet Kahlil Gibran, in his famous work, *The Prophet*, addressed this generation gap. He penned these lines long ago for parents who know little about their own children:

They come through you but not from you,

And though they are with you yet they belong not to you.

You may give them your love but not your thoughts,

For they have their own thoughts.

Parenting today is a lot more about love and letting go and lot less about control and command. Very often as kids grow up, parents stop growing with them. They just grow old.

Mind It!

For movie buffs in India, the expression 'Mind it!' has become synonymous with 'Watch out, here I come!'. It became popular with a hilarious cowboy film of India called, *Quick Gun Murugan*. The hero of the film says something like this in Bollywood Bond fashion, 'The sky is my ceiling. The whole creation is my native place. My name is Murugan, Quick Gun Murugan, Mind it!'

The mind that worships heroic feats on celluloid secretly pines for a life without limitations of space, time and causation. The gun-toting Murugan, like his more celebrated Western counterpart, James Bond, reflects our appetite for flawless control over our mental forces. They are seen to be almost defying the laws of Nature—bending bullets, walking on air and making the impossible possible—with unthinkable ease. Who among us hasn't fantasised about being some kind of a superhuman being sometime or the other? Yet, most of us, when we hit real life outside the movie theatres, just forget about our superhuman status.

Our brain that hosts our mind is divided in many parts like many musical instruments in an orchestra. The right brain is predominantly the synthesiser while the left brain is primarily the analyser. The temporal lobe deals with sounds picked by the ear drum. The billions of neurons inside the brain transmit electrical impulses through little wires called axons. The backbone with its intertwining cable lines supply sensory inputs to the whole brain. The frontal brain, the mid brain and the lower brain—all these brain activities are orchestrated by an unseen conductor called the mind. Mind it! But who really minds the mind?

When you do a mental operation like adding up the price of different items on the shopping list, you are in effect controlling your mental forces through a series of operations in your brain. By confining your thoughts to number crunching, you are making a conscious effort to get the right result after adding the price of items you bought. The one who is making this conscious effort is none else than the conscious you, that can hold your mind by the scruff of the neck, as it were, and make it perform those mathematical tasks.

This is a consciousness that is creatively detached from the mental and emotional forces as well as the physical body. When we identify ourselves with this consciousness rather than with our individual minds and bodies, we can become free from the conditioning limitations of our minds and bodies. We may experience ourselves as a spacecraft that has found an orbit that defies the laws of gravity.

This consciousness has the quality and energy of inner light which the word 'enlightenment' conveys. The sky of consciousness is like a luminous screen on which all the struggles and turmoils of the mind play out. Imagine the white screen in a movie hall on which all the riotous action, suspense and drama are played out. At the end of the movie, the screen still remains unaffected. Our consciousness is like the screen—a luminous witness of our mental, emotional and physical activity. Like the screen, the consciousness is a detached participant in the drama of our life. Unlike the screen, however, this consciousness is not passive but ever alert and creative.

The more we identify ourselves as consciousness rather than as our physical bodies and our chaotic traffic of thoughts and emotions, the more we are able to harness the greater capacities of our mental forces. Our many hidden talents come alive as we are able to channel our mental forces at will with the help of this luminous consciousness. If you consciously know where this genie called your mind is going, you can direct it in ways that it can perform nearly impossible and creative feats.

Coming back to where we started, the verbal excess of Quick Gun Murugan, 'The sky is my ceiling, the whole creation is my native place!' may just be the deeper truth of our ordinary and conscious Self. The search for the heroic that is deeply ingrained in all of us is indeed a search for this omnipresent consciousness that we all are. Murugan simply reminds us of our true identity in his inimitable expression—Mind It!

Would Gandhi Get a Job in a Twenty-first Century Corporation?

One day I fell asleep during one pre-placement talk by the vice president of a company. I dreamt that I was Mahatma Gandhi looking for employment in a twenty-first century corporation. I was wondering if the values of truth and non-violence I had learnt all my life were worthy of today's world. I had applied for a job in the company that the vice president was representing. Let's call this company Complex Lifestyles Solutions Inc. Here is how the conversation went between the Mahatma and the vice president. This dream of mine will tell you that there is so much gap between learning for life and earning for a livelihood.

Dear Mahatma,
On behalf of Complex Lifestyles Solutions Inc, I thank you for applying for the job of Vice President (Corporate

Communications) in our esteemed company. Thank you for sending us your elaborate autobiography.

1. The position you have applied for requires vice not virtue. Please note that we had not advertised for a 'Virtue' President.
2. Your unwavering commitment to truth is dangerous for our organisation's self image. We want someone who can be very, very economical with truth.
3. Here we are looking for a high testosterone, can-do, combat-ready, loud human saxophone and not a turn-the-other-cheek type.
4. We are a socially responsible company as a matter of policy and within permissible limits. We do smuggle some pesticide in our product but make up for it by advertising socially responsible messages on paid commercial channels.
5. You say that you live simply so that others may simply live. Unfortunately, we are in the complex lifestyle solutions business. The more complex life gets, more the people buy our solutions.
6. By the way, what is this ahimsa thing? We are also firm believers in non-violence. We just out-talk, out-smart, out-sell and KILL all competition.
7. Our company mission statement is inspired by one of the greatest leaders in human history who incidentally was born on the same day as you—'There is enough for a man's need but not enough for his greed. As long

as there is never enough, we will continue to be in business.'

We regret to inform you that we cannot offer you the job at the present time. Should a revolution happen in the future, we shall consider.

Sincerely,

VP (Human Re-Engineering)

Dear Vice President,

I realise through my lifelong experiments with truth that it is easier to form perfect vicious circles rather than virtues in cubicles. There is great suffering inside those cubicles where you pretend to work the whole day. Your office spaces look more like stables that house holy cows. There your employees are tied up not by chains but by their tags, titles and designations.

In that boardroom with all the gadgets of the information age, there is still that old culture—'agree culture'. Never mind your obsession with getting the facts on the table and shoving truth under the clean carpet. Your annual reports will make the best of fiction writers blush with envy. They are fabricated for your stake holders who, if they knew the whole truth about your company, will turn into hostile stick holders. Sorry for using a bit of a violent imagination there. Never mind, your future looks as bright as charcoal perched on the back of a water buffalo.

Just the other day, I am sorry to say, I had spotted two of your managers fighting over the size of cushions on their chairs. 'You are merely an assistant manager, how can you have a chair with a thick cushion?' asked the senior guy with bushy eyebrows. As you know it, the boss is always right. A junior's bottom is not eligible for the comfort of a cushy chair. He must suffer his quota of verbal violence and bruised bottom before he gets promoted.

Allow me to sign off with this piece of friendly counsel. Before you sit on your chair every morning, just kneel down in front of it. Then prostrate like you do before a deity, with eight parts of your body touching the floor. Finally focus on the image of the lush leather chair in the sacred space between your eyebrows. You know why? The chair will survive longer in the organisation than you will. Even when you are retrenched and sent home with a pink slip, the chair will look on and smile at you from ear to ear. The chair knows a thing or two about renunciation. It is already preparing to unseat the next Vice President.

Yours truthfully,
Mahatma Gandhi

Education for Ecstasy

The drive to Esalen from San Francisco was magical. The spectacle of the Pacific Ocean coast unfolded like God's own Broadway show. It was my pilgrimage to the source of America's human potential movement that has had a global impact in the fifty odd years that it has existed. Esalen started with its cofounders Michael Murphy and Richard Price in 1962. It quickly became a unique nexus of intellectual and spiritual energy attracting stalwarts such as Abraham Maslow, Joseph Campbell, Fritz Perls and George Leonard, to name a few.

I was invited to be part of a weeklong corporate retreat by Jay Ogilvy, a man with a sharp wit and remarkable intensity in his eyes. He started the retreat in true Esalen fashion urging all of us to 'listen to the ocean' before waves of ideas and insights flooded the Big House where we were staying. The theme of the conference was 'Conscious Capitalism'. Brother David, a well-known teacher, said in jest as in earnest that trying to understand consciousness was like a boy trying to figure out the cause of a toothache. The boy experienced toothache every time he ate sugar. He mistakenly thought that his pain was a result of combination of tooth and sugar. So when his milk tooth fell, he took the tooth to a cube of sugar and wanted to see if that objective contact produced pain. How ridiculous, you may think. How could there be pain without consciousness of the human being who was experiencing the pain? One cannot therefore understand consciousness objectively by being impersonal about it like a scientist. It was evident to me that like the boy with a toothache, one has to experience 'truth-ache' in one's subjective self before one can understand consciousness.

Yet another big idea was that when computer programmes run our world rather than human beings, human response becomes impersonal and unconscious. Many education enterprises are more like real estate businesses. Many schools advertise temperature-controlled swimming pools, swanky buildings with air conditioning and Olympic style running tracks. This seems more like tourism promotion rather than education to me. Making money out of money without creating anything of intrinsic human value is the by-product of unconscious capitalism. When the education business grows beyond the scale and scope of human subjectivity and human comprehension, the world sees monstrous egos emerging out of classrooms.

The answer to the problem of unconscious education is authenticity. When we are authentic, we take off the many costumes that our ego habitually wears. Unfortunately, the business of education thrives on deal making and posturing. 'To be really honest with you, I do not understand what being authentic really means,' said a former principal who was a part of the group. 'Mark your words!' I urged him. 'When you use the expression "to be really honest with you", do you mean to say that you have been dishonest so far? Besides, you don't have to worry about 'being authentic' because pure 'being' is always by its very nature, authentic. When you are being this or being that to fake an identity for gaining some selfish advantage—that's when you trade your authenticity for unconsciousness. That's when you gain a fat salary but lose your contact with your authentic being.'

The Esalen pilgrimage in consciousness would not be complete without the mention of the Esalen communal bathing in natural hot springs, popularly known as 'hot tub'. These hot tubs spout out a few hundred gallons of mineral rich water every minute. It is an elemental, ecstatic feeling in being immersed in one of those tubs with blue sky above and a bluer ocean below. The surging of waves of the ocean hit your eardrums with primordial passion. You visit here to pay homage to the extraordinary human body without discriminating between colour, creed or class. It is here that you can acknowledge the sovereignty of the human body—white or black; woman, man or child—as an expression of the cosmic body without social stigma. It is only then that you awaken to the consciousness of 'Being'—just being without the stress of having to be this or that. For a while you do not have to fit into a sick world in order to be considered healthy. If this is not real education, tell me what is?

Faster is Slower

Nature is a perfect example of the art of waiting. It takes the evolutionary impulse of Nature several thousand years to perfect the shape of a single flower. When we look at natural processes, we realise that there is a certain wisdom hidden in the paradox—faster is slower. How often do we act against the laws of Nature only to realise that we have to make a much greater effort to clean up our mess? In many cultures, patience is misunderstood as plain laziness. However, there is a conscious energy found in patience that provides an impetus towards right action at the right time. Nature demonstrates this day after day.

Only human beings seem to have problems in managing time. No other species on earth suffers from this problem, which is peculiar to our industrial civilisation. The problem of time appears to have emerged with the invention of the clock. The clock is the mother of chronological time. Although it serves a very useful purpose in standardising time around the world, the clock creates a fictitious notion of time as an irreversible, uniform and linear movement of energy.

In Nature, time is never linear; it is cyclical. The laws of Nature clearly tell us that time is reversible. We see the reversal of time in our psychological universe in the form of memory of past events. From the memory of physical Nature, seasons come back year after year, crops grow, the sun rises and sets and the planets go round and round in their orbits.

All ancient civilisations considered time not as an impersonal chronological mechanism measured by a clock, but rather as a living entity that is born, lives and dies like a human being. In India, the word for time is *kala*, which also means death. In the ancient civilisations of South America, there is evidence of the worship of time as a living force. There was a good time and a bad time, an auspicious time and an inauspicious time. People lived in time as they lived in space, avoiding the pitfalls and setting foot on the right time as if it were a bumpy road.

We had laughed away the superstitious beliefs of the ancients until Albert Einstein proved that time, like space, is a relative phenomenon. Because of Einstein we have come to realise that time is not merely determined by the clock but is also manufactured by consciousness. Einstein said, 'Sit with your hand on a hot stove for a minute. It would seem like an hour.' This renewal of the perception of time as a relative phenomenon has taken us back to the wisdom of the ancients, who perceived time as a relative quality rather than an absolute quantity.

In defiance of the modern perception of time as a

chronological journey, it may be said that time is not a one-way public thoroughfare; it is also your living room. I am talking here about personal time. In the context of space, what we see depends on where we sit. In the context of time, our perspective influences how we process time in our consciousness. When our awareness has a chance to expand in time, like when we are in love, time moves at a dizzying speed. When our awareness is constricted in a certain time, like when we are doing an unpleasant chore, time seems to stand still, like a burden on our back. In one of our classroom experiments, we asked some of our students to learn just to sit still in the moment. This task was given to them after they had played a fast paced game of football. The sudden shift from running around the field to having to sit quietly in class was quite a task. The challenge given to them was that they had to bring back their attention to exactly where their own body was sitting. Each time their attention strayed away from their body to someplace else, they had to take notice. Many students reported that they had for the first time observed their wandering minds. Many said that they were thinking of what happened in the football field a few minutes ago. Some others were waiting anxiously for the school bell to ring. In short, they were hardly in the moment in which their body was.

This inability to live in the moment, in the here and now, divorces us from reality. We live in the conceptual time of the clock rather than in the real time of our biological and psychological universe. The stress syndrome that pervades modern classrooms and organisations stems from the fact that in response to external time pressures, we lose our internal harmony. The rhythms of our heartbeat, respiration and hormonal secretions are upset by the mechanical rhythms of networked machines and compulsive pace of the digital world.

When the human brain is fraught with stress and anxiety, our learning capacity is seriously compromised. Stress and anxiety stimulate the bottom half of our mammalian brain that helps us deal with distress. However, this bottom brain is helpful largely in emergency situations, like where to run away from what appears to us a poisonous snake. The top half of the brain, the cortical structure, is where deep learning and understanding take place. When we learn to live in the moment without the chatter of fear or anxiety, our attention is on the top half of the brain. When we operate from this cortical brain, we recognise that what struck us as a real snake is nothing but a plastic toy that was planted by a prankster in school. A brain that stays still in the moment helps us connect with reality of any situation.

Crossing the Circle of Love

Lorna Chopra raised a dimple in her cup of coffee as she whispered, 'I guess love really is blind.' I noticed a mist in her eyes as I said, 'No, love is not blind, attachment that has become addiction is blind.' Lorna was still looking back wistfully at her relationship with her boyfriend. She was mentally back in Mexico as we discussed love in an after-class conversation in suburban France where I was teaching.

In my growing up years in India, the person from whom I had learnt all about love was my grandmother. For her, love meant the joy of letting go. Her favourite fruit was mango. Yet, I hadn't seen her eat a single mango. She would slice delicate crimson-green mangoes with surgical precision for her family. She would watch with indulgent grace as gluttonous guests slurped trickling yellow mango juices off their fingers. Yet, she would not eat a single mango herself! One day I asked her why. She blushed like a ripe Alphonso and with a toothless smile said, 'My husband, when he was alive, loved to eat mangoes more than anything else. When he died, I decided to give up the fruit that I could not share with him.' Long years of silence stretched between her mellowed wisdom and my raw understanding.

I learnt over the years that attachment really blinds you to the greater dimension of love. Letting go was not about losing but about voluntarily moving from the usual addictive appetite to the experience of being truly human. It is better to sometimes lose in love rather than triumph. You know why? Losing gives you a measure of your attachment to the transient.

Like Lorna, many of us see love as an irrational force that is blind to its own follies. Love is not irrational—it goes beyond mundane reasons. Love is its own reason. You cannot define love in geometric precision. Like we say in the world of education, it is worth being approximately right than being precisely wrong. Reason is linear, love is circular. Reason divides and dissects, love unites and multiplies.

In the so called rational world of business education that I inhabit, I have often heard several achievers say, 'I succeed when I love doing what I do.' When I ask them what love essentially is, they fumble and falter. Love is the life breath of all our strivings and all our achievements. I have learnt this expression from Mother Teresa whom I used to know in my Calcutta days. 'It does not matter what you do, unless you are capable of paying deep attention to minute processes in your work, you are unlikely to achieve anything great. Small work with great love is the mantra of micro-excellence.'

A great Yoga teacher of India often exhorts his disciples during the most difficult yoga exercises, 'Put love into your posture.'

'Lorna,' I said, 'Just don't look at love as something you have to hold on to. Rather love is something that takes hold of you and moves you like a free-flowing stream of energy. We must begin to appreciate love beyond our possessive instincts.'

Then I scribbled on a paper napkin a few lines for her.

'You may catch all the petals of a rose, yet you cannot gather its beauty.

You may hold all the water of the river, yet never find its flow.

You may cage a bird, yet not arrest its song.'

A real love story never ends. The real lover never quite loses her beloved because she never possessed him in the first place. A true lover is a lifelong learner. One learns that falling in love happens with all our senses. But when the senses grow weak we have to learn to rise in love through shared wisdom and understanding. As love matures from falling to rising, our learning evolves from sensations to understanding. I once saw an eighty-year-old Indian musician who was deeply in love with his seventy-five-year-old wife. Married for more than fifty years, they barely held hands in public. During one of his concerts, as the music rose to a crescendo, he just glanced at his wife sitting in the audience and they nodded their heads in deep synchronicity. To an onlooker that would seem like the ecstasy of love at first sight.

The Obituary of an Unusual Master

His official name was Soumendranath Mukherjee. A gold medal winner from the Indian Institute of Technology, Kharagpur, he was an all-rounder on campus. After a very successful stint as general manager in a multinational chemical industry Soumenda, as he was popularly known, chose the life of an acharya (a teacher) in an ashram in Deogharh.

Soumenda is unlike anyone I have met before. You may be wondering why I am using the present tense to write this obituary. This is simply because I feel him as a presence so vivid and unmistakeable, just as I did when I met him for the first time. It seems almost inconsequential that I will not see him inside his body anymore. He says in one of our conversations, 'After one has lived a full life, it is best not be too concerned about your body. You have to be prepared to abandon the body like you abandon the bus after you have completed a ride.' How true, if you think of where all our bodies are ultimately going.

Our first meeting happens in his cramped living room in a rundown flat in North Kolkata. Soumenda disarms you with an ear-to-ear smile and that school-kid glitter in his eyes. I have never seen a saint in shorts, let alone someone who wears his sainthood as lightly as a handkerchief that he keeps aside diligently. In our first encounter, he tells me that he is only an unemployed graduate—a BA pass in this spiritual line—waiting for something to happen. The ego-edges that separate one human being from another dissolve in that disarming laughter. His persona leaves you enchanted like an exotic aftershave. You don't even realise that a guru is somewhat like a barber who shaves off excess baggage to show you your bare, naked natural face.

'I cannot claim any spiritual virtues except one,' he whispers to me while chatting up fishermen on the Kapad beach where Vasco da Gama landed in 1498. 'What is that?' I ask. 'I truly see everyone with an equal eye,' he responds as he coaxes a rather coy and thirsty Kerala boatman to drink up a bottle of mineral water so that he could then fill it up with a sample of the Arabian sea. I see the bottle of water gulped down, emptied and refilled again by this boatman who is transfixed by the command. If a sea can be persuaded to get inside a bottle, who am I to believe that a genie called love cannot be bottled up in a human form?

Our two years old Labrador whose name is Mig, takes to Soumenda like a kid takes to another kid. Mig climbs up on Soumenda's neatly prepared bed—occupying space that he does not want to give up without a fight. Soumenda decides to share living and sleeping space with an alien dog. In a day they become fast friends—the dog and his God make peace in an inalienable bond. Mig's primal bark still rings in my heart as Soumenda says goodbye to him in a manner I have never seen him say goodbye before.

Of all my writing Soumenda is fond of this work called *The Circle of Love*. I penned these lines quite some time back in a burst of inspiration. I recognised that the end of all learning is to come back to the source of life. Lesser teachers lead us away from ourselves but the really great ones lead us towards our source self. Learning completes a full circle when at the end of a lifetime's journey we come back to who we truly are. Now, it seems to me that these words of mine can just as well be Soumenda's own:

I shall visit you again in wings of love

floating in the music of the hummingbird.

I shall be there in the first gasp of a new born life

and in the last prayer...

This moment I can write some of my saddest lines. But I hold back knowing that would not be the right way to say bye to a teacher who loved to have the last laugh:

I know you will come back again with the rising of the next tide.

For you are that love we seek,

and you hide.

Until then, farewell.

Alone in Oneness

I sat breathless by the sea shore in Cartagena in the Caribbean Coast of Columbia. The air was filled with the voices of tourists and the puttering of an occasional vehicle. The sun bathed the house of the great writer, Gabriel Garcia Marquez in a sensuous glow. It was a brick red palace presiding over the magical sea. For me, this was a pilgrimage to greatness. I wasn't only thinking of Garcia and *One Hundred Years of Solitude*. I was wondering if one could really become great even when one had no fame or power or just a few pesos in his pocket. Is greatness not born of an inspired heart? What has greatness got to do with the world's approval? Can we all not become great even if we do not win the Nobel Prize like Garcia did?

An olive tanned man imposed himself as my tourist guide as he began to describe how Marquez, now all of eighty years, is writing about the life of a prostitute. How the author's friendship with Fidel Castro of Cuba had earned the anger of many of his countrymen. He pointed towards the house where Marquez and his friends spent time. He shared with me how Cartagena de Indias had been an important port on the Caribbean since it was founded in 1533. Gold and silver left the port bound for Europe. Pirates invaded the city and a walled fort bore testimony of bloody battles and slave trade. Before he could inflict any more history lessons on me, I pressed inside his palm a bunch of pesos, all that I could afford to tell him off. He declined to take the money and made a theatrical bow and thanked me with an unforgettable and exquisite courtesy. I stood humbled by his greatness.

A woman, her hair tied at the end like an arrested black flame, shared a table with me in a seaside café. Her name was Claudia. She had an appointment with me, seeking counsel to get some tips on mending her broken life. Claudia had a translucent, sensuous mouth and oh-so-Venezuelan features. She stretched her finger on the table. On her right index finger was a 'stop light' green emerald that any gemologist in Cartagena would tell you was more precious than their pale green sisters. Colombia, I learned, produced 60 per cent of the emeralds of the world. The Incas and Aztecs of South America, where the best emeralds are found till today, regarded the emerald as a holy gemstone. 'The green of the emerald is the colour of life and of springtime, which comes round in eternal cycles,' I said. Claudia spoke haltingly, 'But it has also, for centuries, been the colour of constant love. In ancient Rome, green was the colour of Venus, the goddess of beauty and love.'

Claudia and I walked towards the sea. She was alone like me.

But, unlike me, she was very lonely. A divorced mother of two children, she said with her eyes fixed on restless waves, 'My life is a waste; I haven't gone anywhere really'. The sea rolled in and rolled away again. 'We come to this world alone,' she sighed, 'and will go back alone.' I said to that, 'Not quite. We are born as one and go back as one. We are one with the world, with the vast solitude of the sea and the mountain; one with the wine flowing from the vineyard and inside our veins; we are one with light inside the emeralds and all the rhythms of the universe. We are born of the great One—the unity of life that courses through our lives—and we will long for the One and merge with the One that is reflected in the seeming multitude of life forms. Listen Claudia, the infinite Oneness is the only secret and the source of all greatness! You are not alone Claudia, you are in the company of your own greatness.'

'*Muchas gracias*. Thank you very much,' Claudia gushed as we concluded our conversation. I blurted out, '*De nada*. You're welcome, don't mention it.' I don't know if Claudia knew that was just about all the Spanish I had picked up from a tourist phrase book in Cartagena.

Measuring the Ocean of Learning with a Paper Cup

Learning is the process of enlarging the limits of our perception. Imagine an ocean that is bottomless and has no defining shores. Our capacity for perception is like that limitless ocean. In the blink of an eye, our perception encompasses the sun, the moon and the stars. We have to do nothing more than open our eyes and the universe is engulfed by our perception. The light of consciousness that makes it possible for us to perceive our universe moves much faster than wind, faster than sound and even faster than solar light.

When this light of consciousness is conditioned by our preconceived ideas about reality, our perceptions become limited. Bringing our limited perceptions to learning is like bringing a small paper cup to measure the depth of an ocean. Think of a glass of blue water that is kept on a table covered by a white cloth under bright sunlight. The water is coloured blue by copper sulphate crystals. As sunlight streams through the glass, it casts a blue glow on the white cloth. One may think that the glow is because of the blue water in the glass. However, if the water is purified and the blue colour begins to fade a little, the sunlight filtering through the water will become clear. It will then become crystal clear that the source of the light glowing on the table is not the water but the Sun. The light of consciousness is like the sunlight. Our preconditioned ideas are like that blue water colouring our perceptions. Unless we remove those filters of conditioned perception, we will not see the light of our consciousness.

Practical Wisdom

I was recently invited by Yale University's Divinity School to deliver a keynote lecture on 'Practical Wisdom'. Practical wisdom is really a contradiction in terms. Wisdom that is not practical is not wisdom at all—dispensing such wisdom is like giving the gift of a comb made of precious ivory to a perfectly bald man.

Wisdom is not a body of codified knowledge that belongs to a certain place or time. Most people confuse the word wisdom with ancient times or something that is of the nature of otherworldly speculation. On the contrary, wisdom has little to do with chronological time. Wisdom is not located in the scattered bodies of knowledge that people dig up through archaeological explorations such as Buddhist stupas or Mayan and Aztec sites. The great irony is that wisdom is not out there—it is within us—in the very source of being human. To look for wisdom outside of us is like a dog chasing its own tail as though it were an external object. Wisdom is that human capacity to see the unity of life in a complexity of forms. What is that practical method through which we can access that unifying intelligence that is inherent in us? There are three principal ways through which we can practice wisdom. They are:

Art of Seeing

The wise ones are known as seers. Seers don't just live in forests like they did in ancient times. They thrive in our corporate jungles, in the sports field and elsewhere. Most people are partial in the way they pick up bits and pieces of impressions from their environment. Most knowledge systems are fragmenting. Most religious and scientific dogmas are fragmenting. But seers are able to see unity in the fragments. They have mastered the art of seeing. Sight is a function of the retina of the eye. Insight comes from a clear mind. Art of seeing is nothing but a clear mind that is not clouded by judgements and emotional drama. This kind of mind has tasted equanimity. Equanimity is the nature of the mind at its depth, just as calmness is the nature of the deep sea. How do we achieve this calmness?

Value of Sharing

One powerful way to achieve this calmness is through unselfish work. When we have less time to think self-obsessive thoughts, we automatically grow calm. The wise grow through sharing. They know that life is indivisible. Life cannot be divided; it can only be multiplied through sharing. In the material universe, life looks like a zero-sum game. If I share one hundred dollars with a friend who really needs it, my dollar wealth is diminished. But my social capital is multiplied, as my capacity to give and serve grows with this gesture. The capacity to give does not come to us automatically; we have to work for it. Bill Gates and Warren Buffet will testify that it is more difficult to give money than to make it. We are born takers. We consume endlessly, soak in affection and care and are awash in avarice. The muscles for giving aren't grown automatically. The wise ones tell us that to give is to live. If we are only for getting, we will be forgotten by the universe.

Alchemy of Silence

Silence is not the economy of speech. Silence is the economy of thought. We think several thoughts in a minute. When we choose to pay conscious attention to our thoughts, they diminish in number. The effect is somewhat like a dense fog becoming lighter as sunlight falls on it. The light of awareness cuts through the fog of excess thoughts. It is not enough to just have thoughts. We have to have the right thought at the right time. Thoughts are not real; they just represent reality in a symbolic form. For thoughts to be effective, they should represent reality as accurately as possible. For this, we must place the right thought in the right context. The alchemy of silence helps us in organising our thought-world with great precision.

Let me illustrate this with a true story. A wise man was invited to receive a prestigious award that is given for bringing peace to our world. As the man was walking towards the grandly decorated stage to receive the coveted prize, a journalist thrust himself before the wise man and asked him, 'Sir, how does it feel to be awarded?'

The wise man smiled at him and taking the next step said, 'I still have a few more steps to go before I receive the award. But this one step towards the stage feels good for sure!'

Other Books by the Author

Timeless Leadership

Leadership Sutras

The Other 99%

Break Free

Circle of Love

Leading Consciously

Light the Fire in Your Heart

Kaun Banega Narayanamurthy
(in Malayalam)

Conversations on Leadership
(Foreword Warren Bennis, Jossey-Bass)

Enciende el fuego en tu Corazón
(in Spanish)

El Liderazgo Consciente: Un Peregrinaje Hacia el Autocontrol
(in Spanish)

Liderance Consciente
(in Portuguese)